God Knows Wl

'Humbled to be reading new book by Sheila Vanessa Leech – *God Knows What I'm Doing Here* – a lady we first met some forty-two years ago – as a young and rebellious drug addict who became a Bible college student, a missionary to Ecuador, a highly qualified nurse, and now director of an emergency international relief mission working in Haiti, Congo-Brazzaville, Lebanon, Pakistan and other war-hit, down-trodden, poverty-stricken corners of the world. An amazing document to God's transforming power and the fruitfulness of a surrendered life. A deeply spiritual yet human story. Compassionate and passionate. Grateful that the family Bowater had a small part at the beginnings of this epic story.'

Chris Bowater OSL; pastor; worship leader; teacher; author; Director, Worship Academy International

'This is a fast, easy, fun, exciting, encouraging, challenging read about a woman from Britain who was called by God to make a difference in the world, and she did it, and continues to do it today. Reading Sheila's story is so inspiring that it will make you wonder what God has for you. The way God has worked through her, in some very challenging situations, is an awesome testimony of the power of simple faith.'

Dr Ron Cline, former President, now Global Ambassador with Reach Beyond

'What can God do with a life that he takes hold of and works through? Anything! Whatever our beginnings, whatever our background, personality or skills, God will use a life given over to serve him. As Sheila's story unfolds you will be drawn into her adventure of walking through life with Jesus. You will be amazed at the variety of experiences an ordinary woman, in the hands of an extraordinary God, can go through and stay sane! I have been moved and challenged by the exploits of Sheila and her friends as they displayed courage and love beyond reason. Surely they could only do what they have done because the love of God compelled them. This is a modern missionary tale that should not be missed. And it is not over yet!'

Elaine Duncan,
Chief Executive, Scottish Bible Society

'Sheila is a masterful storyteller! Once you pick up this book, you won't be able to put it down. With passion and purpose, Sheila eloquently leads you towards a deeper understanding that God is faithful. He can be trusted and he delights to use ordinary people to do extraordinary things!'

Becky Harling,
international speaker and author

'There is hardly anything more fulfilling than serving communities in dire need. Ms Leech makes service to humanity seem less challenging and more inviting through her own exemplary life. From seemingly hopeless and rebellious beginnings, her willingness to serve God and people starts her on an adventurous journey that spans the globe. This book is highly impactful, not only for its ability to open one's mind to various cultures and people, but also for its stout reminder that our faith in Christ, and deeds that reflect that faith, play an important role in transforming the world. Sheila tops this adage with her servant leadership!'

Dilip Joseph, MD, author

God Knows What I'm Doing Here

The incredible story of a mission worker saved from a rebellious past

Sheila V. Leech

Authentic

23 22 21 20 19 18 17   7 6 5 4 3 2 1

First published 2017 by Authentic Media Limited,
PO Box 6326, Bletchley, Milton Keynes, MK1 9GG.
authenticmedia.co.uk

British Library Cataloguing in Publication Data
A catalogue record for this book is available from the British Library.
ISBN: 978-1-78078-452-6
978-1-78078-453-3 (e-book)

Through It All, Andrae E. Crouch
© Copyright 1971, Renewed 1999. Manna Music, Inc./ASCAP
(admin. By ClearBox Rights).
All rights reserved. Used by permission.

Scripture quotations taken from the Holy Bible,
New International Version Anglicised
© 1979, 1984, 2011 Biblica
Used by permission of Hodder & Stoughton Ltd, an Hachette UK company.
All rights reserved.
'NIV' is a registered trademark of Biblica UK trademark number 1448790.

All photos used courtesy of Reach Beyond P.O. Box 39800, Colorado Springs,
CO 80949-9800

Cover design by Mercedes Piñera
Printed in the UK by CPI Group (UK) Ltd., Croydon, CR0 4YY

Contents

Acknowledgements

My grateful thanks to all who feature in this book. There are too many people to mention who have had input into and impact on my life. However, there are some that must be mentioned. Thank you, Ruby Cross, Jan and Neil Crisp, and Gordon and Janet Webb, who walked through the dark, early days with me.

To my church family at Shirley Community Church, I am grateful for your faithful prayers and generous support for thirty-seven years.

To all those who have prayed for and supported me in ministry over all these years and thus actively participated in this ministry.

To Jane Wyllie Vidal, Doreen Villarreal, Bruce and Joyce Moore, heroes of the faith. I trust you are enjoying the presence of the Lord after lives well lived in service to Jesus.

To Sue, Pippa, Karen and Karen (my 'nursie' friends). Your friendship is a special treasure. You make me laugh and are always there for me.

To Karen Cole and Michelle Sonius, I am grateful for your deep friendship and love.

To my brave strong Ecuadorian friends who have travelled the world together and worked shoulder to shoulder to bring hope and healing to those who most need it – Drs Susie Alvear, Eugenia Donoso, Ximena Pozo, Guadaloupe Santamaria, Paola Velez, Paola Estevez and Ivonne Orellana. You are all amazing.

To Dr Steve and Dorothy Nelson, the people I admire most on the planet.

All the staff of Reach Beyond around the world, who day by day sacrifice and give of their time, their energy and their resources so that others may hear about Jesus.

To Jennifer Wood who encouraged me to write this book; her father, Chris Boneham, who came up with the brilliant title; Ralph Kurtenbach who read my early writing; and Huw Spanner who edited so well it became better than I could have imagined.

To members of the International Leadership Team of Reach Beyond past and present – Curt, the best boss in the world, Wolfgang, Ty, Lee, Dan, Simeon, Eric M. I have learnt so much from you all. I am blessed to work with you.

Thank you all.

Finally and most importantly, I want to thank my Lord Jesus Christ for taking a worthless lost soul and giving her a reason to live, a plan and a purpose for life. I am eternally grateful.

Abbreviations

BBI	Birmingham Bible Institute
DRC	Democratic Republic of Congo
HCJB	Heralding Christ Jesus' Blessings. The call letters of a missionary radio station, otherwise known as 'The Voice of the Andes'.
MAF	Mission Aviation Fellowship
RB	Reach Beyond
UNDP	United Nations Development Programme

Part 1

1

Don't Run – They'll Kill You

The tropical rainstorm came on suddenly and in barely a minute the road ahead was under water. The windows of my small pick-up began to steam up and the heat and humidity inside the vehicle quickly became unbearable. I opened my window to let in some cooler air and my arm and shoulder were soon soaked by the pouring rain. I could see only a few yards ahead, if that, but at least I knew that the next few miles of road were, by Ecuadorian standards, in good repair.

I was now driving slowly but as I rounded a bend I felt the tyres slip and the vehicle begin to aquaplane. I slowed even more and thought with a sinking heart of the long road ahead of me. Many hours of driving lay before me, climbing from sea level to ten thousand feet before snaking through the Andes Mountains to Quito, the capital. It is a beautiful route through spectacular scenery, but there is nowhere to stop for a rest, or even to get petrol, for the first four hours. I had travelled this road, from San Lorenzo on the north-west coast of Ecuador, just a few miles from the Colombian border, many times before and its emptiness never bothered me. Usually, I relished the idea of some hours alone in the car when I could think about God, my work and life in general. However, the prospect of making the trip in torrential rain didn't have quite the same appeal!

At that time Reach Beyond, the mission agency I work for, ran a blindness-prevention project in San Lorenzo and my job as director of its community development department required me to go there once a month. On the way down from the mountains the day before, the going had been good and I had made the journey in a record five hours. My meetings at the eye clinic had gone better than expected and I was feeling refreshed after a good night's sleep and eager to get back to Quito. Now, though, the rain dashed my hopes for a quick and enjoyable drive home. My greatest fear was that it would cause landslides that would make the road impassable both in front of me and behind me. I didn't want to get stuck overnight and I breathed a silent prayer, asking God to get me back safely.

And then, as abruptly as it had started, the rain stopped. It was as if someone had drawn a line on the road where the downpour was to end. I wound down all the windows and began to relax as cooler air blew through the vehicle with the fresh, moist scents of the rainforest. A toucan flew suddenly across the road in front of me, its wings flapping furiously as if that were necessary to carry the weight of its great yellow beak, which stuck out straight ahead. I burst out laughing at the sight and my heart was lightened as I took in the beauty of the lush tropical forest and the wildlife God had created to live there. I reflected on how quickly things could change in Ecuador, from the weather to the scenery – and even the currency and the president! – and I thanked God for the privilege of living in such a beautiful and varied country. Life was certainly never boring.

An hour passed quickly. The winding road became much rougher, but nothing could spoil my pleasure as I drove. I looked forward to getting back to my home in Tumbaco, on the outskirts of Quito, where my housemate and her parents,

who were over from the United States, would be waiting for
me. Don and Dixie Weaver were regular visitors to Ecuador,
where their daughter, Jane, was a missionary surgeon. I loved
spending time with them and now I was looking forward to a
relaxing evening with delicious food and good conversation.

Rounding a bend, I had to brake sharply as an unexpected
obstruction came into view. At first glance, I thought that a
large articulated lorry had jackknifed. The road was completely
blocked, and a jam of buses, trucks and cars was waiting to get
past. I briefly thought of turning round and going back to San
Lorenzo and taking the coastal road to Quito, but the thought
of the extra eight hours' driving it would entail soon changed
my mind. Surely, it wouldn't be long before the way ahead was
clear. I pulled up behind a bus, on the right side of the road –
though, in typical Ecuadorian style, the whole width of the
tarmac was now a jumble of vehicles waiting to slip through
the first gap that opened.

As I reached to turn off the ignition, I noticed a man walking
down the road towards me. He looked like a typical local
farmer, short in stature, with black hair and brown skin. He
was wearing a khaki shirt, loose over a pair of blue jeans, long,
black rubber boots and a floppy bush hat. As he approached,
it occurred to me he was going to ask me for a lift, perhaps to
the nearby town of Lita. My usual policy is not to give lifts to
strangers when I travel alone and I had begun to debate with
myself whether I should let him ride on the back of the pick-up
when he walked up to my window.

To my horror, I saw that he was pointing a gun at me! It
looked huge. As I come from England I'm not used to seeing
handguns, and have never handled one in my life. This one
looked like the kind of thing cowboys carry in Wild West
movies: it was silver, with a white grip, and had chambers

which I knew held real bullets – and it was aimed at me! Suddenly I realized what was happening. The truck up ahead had not broken down; this was a hold-up! I had often read in *El Comercio*, one of the local newspapers, about robberies on Ecuador's more remote roads, where robbers would block the road to stop interprovincial buses and trucks and would hold the drivers and passengers at gunpoint while they took their money and jewellery and other valuables. Usually this happened at night, however. To run into it in broad daylight was a huge shock.

As I stared at the barrel of that gun, I felt the blood draining from my face. My heart was racing, my mouth was dry and there was a ringing sound in my ears. I couldn't believe this was happening to me. The man appeared to be in his late twenties or early thirties and didn't seem overly aggressive or violent – in fact, he didn't fit my image of a bandit at all. I have no recollection of what he said to me, but I know he instructed me to pull over to the other side of the road, alongside a second bus, and my hands and feet obeyed him automatically.

He asked me politely to get out of the pick-up and searched me. I was wearing jeans and a tee shirt with boots and I had nothing in my pockets. The only 'jewellery' I had on was a watch, a silver cross on a chain and my everyday earrings. As he patted me down, I told him: '*No tengo nada*, I have nothing.' I watched him search the vehicle methodically, opening the glove compartment and checking under the sunshade and then going through my personal belongings. My mind was racing as I tried desperately to remember what was in my overnight bag. My first thoughts were of my passport, my cellphone – useless in that part of the country because there is no reception – my driver's licence, my credit card and a small amount of cash. Bizarrely, I found myself trying to work out how I would get back to Quito with no money for petrol and no papers to show at the police checkpoints.

As he continued his search, I looked around. The people in the bus were staring through the windows with expressions of concern on their faces. Two men were making signs and mouthing: '*No corres!* Don't run! *Te matarán*, they'll kill you.' They drew their fingers across their throats for emphasis. Maybe they thought I didn't understand Spanish, but their sign language was certainly graphic.

The sound of tearing paper brought me back to the moment and I remembered with a start that I had two sealed manila envelopes in the back of the cab, full of receipts and cash from the clinic. I reckoned that money and possessions could always be replaced, but I silently called out to God to spare my life!

Once the man had finished, he told me to get back into the vehicle and shut the door. The look of astonishment on his face when I asked him if I could go had to be seen to be believed! He could barely suppress a smile as he told me: 'No, *señora*, you have to stay here until two o'clock. *Pero tranquila!* Be calm!'

After he left, I looked down at my belongings strewn about the cab. It looked as if he had left most of my things. I wanted to check to see what he had taken but I felt I should just keep my hands in view and stay calm. My pulse had slowed a little and my breathing was less agitated as I realized that for the present my life had been spared. But for how long?

My heart began to race again when I noticed that there were many armed men around and the others had ski masks over their faces and were carrying automatic rifles. They had deliberately positioned the vehicles so that they could move between them without being seen, so that it was impossible to tell how many men there were, or where they were at any given moment. It dawned on me that these were no common criminals. I guessed that the innocent-looking man who had searched my pick-up was dressed like a farmer to allay suspicion as each new driver arrived at the hold-up. These men were obviously well-disciplined and well-rehearsed. There were no raised voices, no arguments. All their victims were sitting in their vehicles in absolute silence.

I felt a sense of dread, not knowing what might happen next. It was getting hotter as the sun climbed higher into the sky, and perspiration broke out on my forehead. The silence seemed eerie, broken only by the whirr of insects and the screech of an occasional parrot in the surrounding rainforest. Every now and then, someone fired a gun into the air as a reminder that these men were serious and wouldn't hesitate to use their weapons.

Time crawled by as I sat there in the tropical heat, surrounded by the most spectacular scenery but in absolute terror for my life. I'd decided that our assailants were Colombian rebels and I was afraid that I might be abducted and held for ransom, as so many other foreigners had been before. I started to compose a speech in Spanish that would explain that I was a missionary and nobody would pay anything to free me; that I ate a lot and would probably get sick; and that it would therefore be better to kill me straight off rather than kidnapping me!

Once I had this speech off pat, my mind began to drift and I started to think about what had brought me to Ecuador in the first place . . .

2

A Teacher's Prayer

I was born in the late fifties and grew up in the small Warwickshire village of Bentley Heath, where our family of eight was known by just about everyone. You couldn't get away with any misdemeanours of any description, it was that kind of a place. The nearest town was Solihull, 3 miles away, and the second largest city in England was about 15 miles; but they might as well have been 100 miles away. We rarely went to Solihull and we visited Birmingham only once a year, for the children's Christmas party that my dad's employers held. Everything we needed and wanted was right there in our village.

Our world consisted of the local shops (a greengrocer, a butcher, a hair salon, a post office and a sweet shop which also sold newspapers), the park, our school (Dorridge County Infant and Junior), the small dairy where my dad worked and the fields surrounding the village where we roamed at will, learning to catch sticklebacks in the small streams and swimming in the River Blythe. The recreational fields ('the rec') were the setting for games of football in the winter and cricket, tennis and rounders in the summer. For us children, the high points of the week were 'the Tuesday meeting', a kids' club held at the local Brethren church, and the arrival of the 'chip wagon' (a mobile fish 'n' chip shop) every Wednesday. Just about every child in the village looked forward to these two important occasions, me and my five siblings included.

I am number five in our family. The three boys came first, followed by three girls. The arrival of my older sister, Rosemary, had been a huge relief for my mum and dad after so many sons! She was all a parent could wish for in a baby – blond curls, green eyes and a peaches-and-cream complexion – and my brothers adored her. My arrival was a disappointment, I'm sure – I have dark hair and eyes and sallow skin and was certainly not a pretty child. My younger sister, June, followed two years later and my mum declared that she was definitely the last, so she had a special place as the baby of the family. She also got the genes for blond hair and paler skin.

As I grew up, it became clear that I'd got the tomboy genes. I loved nothing more than climbing trees, riding my bike and kicking a football around with my friends. A big group of us spent our summers building dens and tree-houses and generally playing out of doors. I had no interest whatsoever in knitting, sewing or doing puzzles – or any kind of 'sitting down' activity. My knees were rough and grazed and my fingernails usually held 'enough dirt to grow potatoes', as Dad used to say.

I was baptized into the Catholic church as an infant, but once my maternal grandmother had passed away, when I was still quite small, religion didn't feature much in our family life. Grandma Carney had ruled our family. My dad had been raised a Methodist but was required to convert to Catholicism if he wanted to marry my mum. Grandma Carney imposed her Irish Catholic beliefs on my brothers and insisted that they attend Mass and go to a Catholic school. She was extremely devout. She never missed Mass on a Sunday and went even on her last day on earth, despite feeling unwell. She had a massive heart attack on the steps of Our Lady of the Wayside church and died a few hours later.

After that, my religious instruction passed to the local Brethren assembly, which ran a Sunday school, the Tuesday meeting and weekly covenanter classes. Tuesday evenings were a lot of fun: we enjoyed organized games and competitions, and every year there was an outing to St Nicholas Park in nearby Warwick, which boasted an outdoor paddling pool and a Peter Pan railway. At Sunday school, you could win prizes for perfect attendance and from time to time we were treated to 'Fact and Faith' films and films of Billy Graham's evangelistic 'crusades'.

In among all these activities, we listened to Bible stories, memorized verses of Scripture and learnt how to pray. Above all, we were taught that we were all sinners who needed God's forgiveness for all the things we'd done wrong, but that Jesus had come and died on the cross to take the blame for our misdeeds. I knew the gospel at an early age – but it had no impact on my life.

My Sunday-school teacher, Mrs Wood, regarded me as a 'naughty' child. I was rude and disruptive, I talked too much and I argued, and even fought, with the other kids. Many years later, when I was talking to her as an adult, she confessed that she used to mention me in her prayers every week. She would plead with God, 'Please don't let Sheila Leech come to class today! Please keep her away!'

One day, I got into a serious fight with one of the other girls. Our teachers had to pull us apart as we kicked and punched each other and one of them said to me as I cried with rage, 'There's only one person who can help you now!' I knew she was referring to Jesus. I'd been taught that when life was difficult and seemed unfair, he would always be there to comfort me, heal me and forgive me. 'I know,' I said angrily, 'and I don't want him!' With that, I turned my back on God and walked out of the door, and it would be many years before

I ever set foot in a church again. However, I should say that although I turned my back on God that day, he never turned his back on me.

After that, my increasingly rebellious lifestyle led me to make many poor choices and serious mistakes. My mum used to say I had 'got in with the wrong crowd', but the truth was that I was *one* of the wrong crowd. I drank heavily. I took drugs, and began stealing in order to pay for them. By the time I was seventeen I had become someone that no respectable person wanted to be seen with, let alone spend time with. One day, I was walking down the high street in Solihull with a group of friends when I saw my sister Rosemary coming towards me with some of her friends. I was wearing filthy jeans and boots as always and my hair was tangled and greasy. As I stumbled along in a drug-induced haze, it must have been obvious I had been sleeping on the streets. My sister walked past me without so much as a second glance, too embarrassed even to acknowledge me.

(I have to say, though, that my other sister was always kindness itself. Whenever I came home in a bad state, June would remove my boots, help me to bed and cover me up, never once asking me where I had been or what I'd been up to.)

One particularly excruciating experience was my premature departure from Tudor Grange Grammar School for Girls. I had managed to get some O-levels and was in the Lower Sixth when my parents were summoned to meet the headmistress. The outcome of that meeting was not exactly expulsion but an agreement that I would not return. My behaviour at school and my 'extracurricular activities' had been having a bad effect on others and bringing the name of Tudor Grange into disrepute.

Once I left school, my life seemed to spiral downwards out of control. I wandered around, lost and lonely, strung out on drugs and alcohol. I was constantly trying to sort myself out.

I would stay with different friends, a night here, a night there. My parents were beside themselves – they couldn't understand why I was behaving this way. How had I got into such a mess, they asked – and why? As long as I was with my mates I held myself together, but once I was alone I was the saddest soul on the planet. I felt that my life was not worth living.

I rode a motorcycle and most evenings I could be found in a pub with a group of bikers in black leather jackets and boots. One Friday, I was in a pub in Solihull town centre, hanging out with the bikers, when a strange group of people walked in. They were wearing smart shirts and trousers and some even had ties on – and they were carrying large, black Bibles. Word went around that they were something to do with the police or the probation service, but when I spoke with them I learnt that they were there just to talk to the people in the pub and give them a simple message: God loves you, and Jesus died on the cross so that you can be forgiven for all the things you've done wrong.

Their visits became weekly events and what they told us never changed. It brought back to me memories of Sunday school and the message I had heard there all those years ago. I remember one particularly emotional discussion with two of the group one evening. I just couldn't believe that God loved me. Yes, for sure he loved people like them – clean and shiny and smiling with their big Bibles – but me, with my unwashed hair, my filthy jeans, my dirty leather jacket and smelly boots – and my bad attitude?

One thing that struck me about this group was that they didn't just talk about God's love, they also demonstrated it by doing very practical things to help us. They would invite us into their homes and give us strong black coffee and food; they would even bail people out if they were arrested. As I witnessed their genuine kindness and concern, I began to ask myself: Why are they doing all this? Can their message be true? Can God love someone like me? Can he really – will he really – forgive someone like me for all the things I have done and said – for my thieving and cheating, my violence, my lies, my loose morals? A glimmer of hope was born in my heart. What if it were true? Could there be a different life for me? Was there a future for me?

Around this time, one of my friends who had gone missing for a while turned up in the pub. Steve had been a heavy drinker and drug user, but now he seemed very different. Clean, clear-headed – just very different! I guessed that he'd been to prison and had benefited from a few months of decent food and no drugs, but the story he told us was not at all what I'd expected. He began to tell us about an amazing change that had taken place in him. He had been at a very low point, he said, when he'd met someone who had told him about Jesus and how he could 'turn him around' and give him a new direction and purpose.

Steve said he had 'committed his life to God', asked him to forgive him for his sins and received what he called 'a new life'. Now he was free from drugs and alcohol, and was going to church. In fact, his sole reason for coming to the pub was to see his old mates and invite us to come to his church the next Sunday, when he would be telling the whole congregation about his transformation – what he called 'giving his testimony'.

That invitation was accompanied by another one, to have supper at his house that Sunday evening. A few of us agreed to go and I think that offer of a meal was the deciding factor! I myself had not stepped inside a church for many years and part of me was a bit apprehensive about going into what I felt would be a strange and even hostile environment. My lifestyle in those days was just so far removed from the clean, hushed halls of the Brethren assembly I'd attended as a child.

However, the 'church' turned out to be a community hall, and the service was unlike anything I'd ever experienced. There was a group of people playing guitars and drums, and a warm, friendly atmosphere – the people actually looked pleased to see us! After a few lively songs – not hymns – Steve told his story. It really impressed those of us who had known him previously. He'd certainly changed. He looked different, he sounded different and there was a new liveliness about him. It seemed he had found a reason to live, a sense of purpose, a hope! The truth of his words was visible in his face and his demeanour.

After that, a small man stood up. He was almost as wide as he was tall, with a ruddy complexion and a shock of pure white hair. He stood at the lectern and for the next half-hour he talked about – well, me! He seemed to know all about me and my lifestyle, my wrongdoing and even the misery and desperation I felt when I was alone. He looked straight at me as he banged the lectern and talked in a loud voice about 'sinners' who 'need to get right with God', whose only hope of salvation was 'being in a right relationship with Jesus Christ'.

At least, that's what I think he said. The truth is, my heart was beating so hard that I could barely hear him. Something was happening to me. I could hardly breathe. I wanted to look away from this odd little man but I couldn't. I knew that he knew all the terrible things about me, where I had been and what I had done. Who had told him? Steve? I wished I could get out of there.

Eventually, he was done – almost. He asked everyone to close their eyes to pray and, for what seemed an excruciatingly long time, he invited those who wanted to receive God's forgiveness and start a new life to raise a hand. His appeal went on and on; my heart was racing, I was hyperventilating and felt faint and nauseous. When it was over, I rushed to the door of the hall, desperate to escape, only to find my way blocked by this man who apparently knew all about me. He put out his hand to shake mine and looked into the very depths of my soul, so it seemed, and saw me. He invited me to come again and said he would be praying for me.

The sense of relief when I got out of that building and away from those people was overwhelming. Their kindness, love and acceptance were simply too much for me. Their cleanness challenged me – there was something so innocent, pure and uncomplicated about them. They seemed so genuine, whereas I felt contaminated inside.

Nonetheless, over the next two years I went back several times, albeit infrequently. It was as if a magnet was pulling me to that church. I went to the Sunday evening 'gospel' service and each time I heard the same message, that Jesus loves sinners, that he died on the cross to take our punishment, that he wants us all to turn from our sin and come to him to receive his gift of forgiveness and a new life. 'There is no catch, and nothing you need to do except come.'

Whenever I heard that message, my heart would leap with hope. Could it be true? Could God's grace be extended even to someone whose life had gone as bad as mine? Who 'the system' had given up on? Who at times didn't even want to go on living? Could a sinner like me be forgiven? Even me?

One weekend, one of the young people from the church invited me to stay in her parents' beautiful home and go to church with her on the Sunday. Having nothing better to do, I agreed. I had never attended a Sunday-morning service there before. It was a communion service and most of the prayers and readings were concerned with Jesus' sacrifice of himself on the cross. There was a point in the service when anyone could say a prayer or sing something or share a verse of Scripture that was meaningful to them, and over and over again people were standing up and thanking Jesus for his willingness to suffer and die in order to secure our forgiveness – my forgiveness – from God.

Something happened to me then, something so strange, so unexpected, and so wonderful I will never forget it. I felt embraced by an amazing sense of God's love. I felt overwhelmed by it, as if it were all around me – as the hymn-writer says,

O the deep, deep love of Jesus,
    vast, unmeasured, boundless, free!
Rolling as a mighty ocean
    in its fullness over me!
Underneath me, all around me,
    is the current of Thy love,
leading onward, leading homeward
    to Thy glorious rest above![1]

That love was palpable – I could see it, smell it, touch it, taste it and hear it. In that moment, I knew it was true that God loved me. I began to weep – I felt like my heart was shattering into a thousand pieces. I had come into that church as a 'hard' biker in a black leather jacket, jeans and boots. I was someone who never cried. But now I couldn't hold back or hide my tears. I had no handkerchief to mop my eyes or wipe my streaming nose. My heart was bursting at the realization that finally I had found what I had been searching for, for so long. Except it was not a 'what' but a 'who'.

Pastor Bowater, that small powerhouse of a preacher, was very sensitive to the Holy Spirit's leading, and he sensed that

God was dealing with a few people in the church that morning. He waited for an appropriate moment and then he invited the congregation to bow their heads and close their eyes. He asked if there was anyone who wanted to commit their life to Christ. My hand shot into the air. After all, I thought, no one except the pastor could see me. 'God bless you, Sheila!' he said. Even worse was to come. At the end of the service, he invited all those who had raised their hands to go up to the front of the church to be prayed for.

Nonetheless, when I walked out of that little church that Sunday morning I felt I was walking on air. I knew I was a new person, totally and utterly changed. Forgiven and clean. What a feeling!

I want to end this story there. I want to say that I went on to be a happy, victorious Christian who never touched drugs again. I want to say that I lived a pure and blameless life, reflecting the beauty of Jesus and extending his grace to others. I want to say that, but it wouldn't be true. The truth is that the next six months were some of the hardest and darkest in my life to that point. Just days after that wonderful experience, my dad was diagnosed with cancer. His prognosis was not good. Shortly after that, I was arrested for something I had done eight months earlier. Where was God now? In my immaturity, I'd imagined that somehow as a Christian I had a 'get out of jail free' card and all life's troubles were over. I was sorely disappointed. I felt that God had let me down.

It took a further six months of downward spiral before I hit rock bottom. Finally, I gave up trying to do things by myself and then, at last, God intervened and in a miraculous way began to build my new life.

3

The Only One Who Can Help

My conversion to Christianity – or decision for Christ, or surrender to God or whatever you want to call it – was dramatic. Walking to the front of the little church that Sunday morning, I felt my heart break and then fill with overwhelming peace and a sense of forgiveness – yes, and joy. I felt clean. I *knew* I was forgiven – and I *felt* forgiven: unburdened, light and positive. I was determined to turn my back on the sordid life I'd been living. I learnt later that the Bible calls this 'repentance'. Right then, I just felt that I needed to brace myself and work hard to be different.

And how hard I did try – and how badly I failed! Nowhere in the teachings of Jesus are we encouraged to pull ourselves up by our own bootlaces. It's impossible. We cannot change ourselves – that is God's work. It is his Spirit, living and working in our hearts, who makes the difference. We are required only to yield to God and let him have free rein in our lives. He is the one who brings about lasting change – the kind of change I longed for.

I spent six months trying to 'do the right thing'. Then I gave up. I was exhausted by the struggle and disheartened by my continual failure to stop taking drugs. I started to think that maybe this 'Christian life' thing was just not for me. Maybe

I was too hard for God to change. Maybe even he had given up on me.

At just the right time – God's time – some people re-entered my life who could help me. Jan Crisp had been one of my Sunday-school teachers – in fact, she was the one who had tried to point me to God after the fist fight with that other girl. 'You know there's only one person who can help you?' she said to me now, and it was as if the years had fallen away and I was back in my childhood. Her question was also an invitation. I looked into her bright, blue eyes and saw kindness and compassion. She is a feisty woman married to a calm and godly man, a combination of personalities that for over sixty years has helped to bring many people into the kingdom.

I was nineteen years old and sitting in Jan's kitchen, eating flapjack and drinking coffee. The Christian world around Bentley Heath is small and she and Neil had heard about my troubles and had been praying for me. Not only that, but they had been looking for some kind of rehabilitation centre where I could get specialist help. Now they believed they had found the right place and they wanted me to go with them to take a look.

It was a warm July evening when we set off for Hill Farm. We didn't talk much in the car – I had nothing to say. I thought there was nothing in life worth living for and I had given up. I felt now that I was being propelled towards the inevitable, whatever that might be. I had no will either to resist or agree to their plan.

We arrived at our destination an hour later and turned into a long driveway. I was oblivious to the beauty of the surroundings: the rolling green Worcestershire hills, the golden fields ready for harvest, the dahlias that brightened the edges of the drive. None of it made any impression on me. We pulled into the yard and I saw a big farmhouse and an old timbered barn, with stables on three sides. There was also a large brick building, set slightly back from the yard, that looked much newer than the others.

The door of the house opened and four people came out. Bryan and Carol, Francis and Mary were the two Christian couples who now ran the centre. I later learnt that Bryan had been a heroin addict and had gone through rehab there a few years earlier. He had subsequently gone to Bible college, where he had met Carol, and later they and their 3-year-old daughter, Sarah, had come to run the centre. Francis and Mary were a gentle couple. He had a wonderful, rich Devon accent. He was responsible for the farming side of things as well as sharing the leadership with Bryan. He and Mary had one, beautiful child, Joshua, who soon became a favourite with me.

I don't remember much about that first evening, but as I was in effect homeless it was not a difficult decision when they invited me to stay for the weekend. I had spent the last twenty-four hours with Jan and Neil and hadn't taken any drugs for some time, so I wasn't expecting a good night's sleep. My new hosts explained that the modern brick building was actually the principal accommodation for their guests, but as all the others were men I would be staying in the farmhouse with the two families.

They gave me a nightgown, a toothbrush and a towel and showed me to my room. Not knowing what else to do, I got undressed and lay down on my bed, waiting for the effects of withdrawal to start. Meanwhile – as I found out later – Bryan, Carol, Francis and Mary gathered downstairs to pray. All night.

I was awoken by the sun streaming through the window. I lay for a few moments wondering where I was. I was used to waking up in all sorts of different places and it was a relief to find I was alone, with four walls around me and, by the looks of things, clean and safe. An overwhelming sense of fatigue overcame me, and it was a struggle to get up and dress. My one thought was to get away from that place – I needed to find some drugs. To my surprise, the sun was high in the sky. I had slept for more than twelve hours.

I made my way out of the house and started to walk slowly down the drive, which seemed interminable. Within minutes, I was gently apprehended by Mary, who had spotted me from a window 'making my escape'. She took my arm and guided me back to my room, where I slept, again. This pattern – of sleep, attempted escape and interception – was repeated several times over the next couple of days.

Soon, I started to be awake more often than I was asleep. I began to explore the farm and find out about the other residents. They were an eclectic group. Most of them had had serious drug habits and some were also struggling with alcoholism. All of them had at some point reached rock bottom and cried out to God. All of them had experienced his power, his love and his forgiveness.

After four days at the farm, I was invited to a meeting with Bryan and Francis. Some issues needed to be discussed, they said. The main question was whether or not I wanted to stay. This was a pressing question since I was on probation and had to advise my probation officer of any change of address or other alteration in my circumstances. Any delay in informing him might land me back in court.

Bryan spelt out the conditions for staying at Hill Farm. The first one shocked me: I had to commit to stay for at least a year. A *year*? I thought: That's like forever! He explained that it normally takes at least a year to get someone to make a complete break with their old lifestyle and friends and stay clean. He added that I shouldn't go back to the Solihull area and my friends there for about four years. I was flabbergasted. I couldn't imagine not seeing my mates for four years. I began to cast around for ways around these rules, with a succession of questions that began, 'What about if . . . ?'

Bryan knew just how to deal with these. As an ex-addict himself he knew exactly what I was thinking. He told me that if I decided to stay, I would be making a commitment not to the staff, not to the other residents, not to Jan and Neil but to God himself. I would be promising God that I was determined to change and would do whatever was necessary to co-operate with him in that process.

This changed the picture completely. This was serious. I started to feel uncomfortable. My mind was racing as a battle began to rage in my head. I wanted to grasp this lifeline but I could feel an almost physical pull back to my old life. I realized that this was one of the most important decisions I would ever make and a feeling of panic came over me. I had an urge to escape, quite literally – I wanted to run. Bryan saw my distress and he started to pray, asking God to bring peace to my heart.

Within minutes, I felt a new calmness in my mind and my spirit. I began to breathe more easily. I've noticed many times that when things feel out of control or my life is in danger, a battle begins in my head, between focusing on my plight and trusting God. When I fix my thoughts on the Lord Jesus, I'm at peace. When I consider my situation, I panic. I'm reminded of Peter in Matthew's Gospel when he walks across the water towards Jesus. When he fixes his eyes on him, he stays up; when he looks down at the waves, he begins to sink. One of my favourite verses in the Bible is 'You will keep in perfect peace those whose minds are steadfast, because they trust in you' (Isaiah 26:3). Many times that battle has raged as I've struggled to keep my mind stayed on the Lord Jesus.

At the end of the meeting, I went back to my room. I needed to think about what had been said and to ponder all the other rules Bryan had told me – no leaving the farm unaccompanied for six months, no visitors, attendance at church, attendance at devotions, no missing meals, a full day's manual work every day and so on. I sat in my sun-filled room that afternoon, alone and yet knowing I wasn't alone, indecisive yet knowing the decision had already been made. I found peace even though I felt like I was standing at the edge of a cliff. What would it mean to live my life for God and with God? I had no idea. Would I have to do things I hated? Would I have to give up all the things I loved? Without any answers to those questions, I took a deep breath and jumped.

Life at Hill Farm quickly became a familiar routine. We gathered each morning for Bible study, music and prayer. The leaders of our community knew that our only hope of getting and staying clean was to cultivate a lively relationship with God, and they believed that the way to do that was to spend time with him in prayer, reading the Bible and enjoying fellowship with other believers.

We spent the rest of the day doing particular jobs around the farm. Francis's vision was that the centre should be self-sustaining – that is, it should produce all we needed to eat, with enough left over to sell to pay the utilities bills and buy the necessities the farm didn't produce. There wasn't much livestock. Priscilla, a beautiful Guernsey cow, gave us rich, creamy milk to drink, and what was left over we churned into butter and cream. A white goat called Gertie was also milked twice a day, and her offspring, Rameses and Bertram, involuntarily supplied us with meat. We also kept hens for their eggs and farmed the land to grow potatoes, carrots, turnips and cabbages. There was a harvest of apples in the autumn and we gathered blackberries along the hedgerows around the farm.

It would have been an idyllic existence had it not been for the fact that each of us was struggling with our own personal issues. Sometimes, the frustration – or desperation – would become obvious. Some of the residents left and we never heard from them again. Others were so damaged they would probably never be able to live independent lives. Some, however, were well on their way to being able to return to 'normal' life, whatever that would turn out to be for them.

I had my particular struggles. I was naturally a rule-breaker and I found it hard to live in such a disciplined environment. This got me into trouble on a number of occasions – and it would have been worse had it not been for the arrival of Ruby, which proved to be one of the best things that ever happened to me. From my very first day at Hill Farm, I had been told that she would soon be arriving, a single woman coming fresh from Bible college to join the team. Her principal responsibilities would be cooking and housekeeping. As I was the only female resident and the only other women on site were Carol and Mary, everyone thought it would be nice for me to have another single woman around, though I wasn't so sure.

Ruby had had a very sheltered upbringing, having grown up in the Orkney Islands, off the north-east coast of Scotland. She was born on a very small island but had lived on the 'mainland' of Orkney for most of her life. She had attended Birmingham Bible Institute with Bryan and Carol and they had encouraged her to pray about joining the team at Hill Farm. Previously, she had gone to cooking school in Aberdeen and had later become the chief housekeeper at the hospital on Orkney. She was said to be an excellent cook.

Our first mealtime with her, when she eventually arrived, was memorable. No one spoke to her. Poor Ruby! She was naturally shy, she had travelled by ferry and overnight train to reach the farm and she was exhausted. Finding herself for the first time among a group of drug addicts, a long way from her family and friends, she felt very uncomfortable – especially as none of them would speak to her! It wasn't that nobody wanted to speak, but small talk, especially with strangers, was immensely hard for most of the residents. Carol and Mary tried their best to start a conversation around the table but to no avail. Ruby later confessed to me that it was the worst mealtime of her life.

Before long, however, her genuine warmth and goodness became apparent to all. She was kindness personified: selfless, hardworking and almost saintly. Yes, she had a strange accent, yes, she was incredibly naive, but before long she and I became great friends, and she was a true mentor to me. I thank God to this day for Ruby Mowat (now Mrs Ruby Cross). She was the person I looked to for guidance and turned to for comfort and advice, and from whom I got my standards of Christian behaviour.

Our relationship was stormy at times – usually as a result of my refusal to face reality and deal with it, and Ruby's desperation that I shouldn't mess up completely. My rebellious spirit led me to flout the rules openly, and at times this brought Bryan's wrath down on me. There was one occasion when he and Francis seriously discussed whether I should be allowed to stay. I had escaped from the farm and hitchhiked into Solihull, where I managed to buy some drugs. Ruby scoured the pubs with some Christian friends until they finally found me, stoned. She sneaked me back into the farm after we'd sat in her car in the road until all the lights had gone out. Her intercession on my behalf the next day was probably a significant factor in the leadership's decision to give me one last chance.

Being the only young, single woman not on the staff was a challenge. I wasn't allowed to leave the farm on my own and when I did go outside it was always as part of a group going to church or doing some Saturday afternoon evangelism in the nearby town of Redditch, where we handed out leaflets and engaged people in conversations about God. There was rarely an outing that was purely for fun. Ruby soon sensed that I would benefit hugely from a shopping trip to town, so occasionally she would take me along with her on her day off. I loved these excursions, because they made me feel that I was normal again and not just one of the 'Hill Farm residents', as we were known.

She also managed to persuade Bryan and Francis to let me help her in the kitchen one day a week. The outdoor work on the farm was tough and tiring and it was a joy to stay in the relative warmth of the kitchen, peeling potatoes, washing dishes or helping Ruby bake. I also had my regular tasks each day, which included milking Priscilla and Gertie by hand and cleaning out their stalls. I loved these chores. I would lean my head against Priscilla's warm flank as I worked and often would confide in her my feelings of anger, frustration and sadness. That cow never betrayed any of my secrets.

Each Thursday evening, we had an open evening so that family, friends and people from the local churches could visit. We enjoyed times of singing and testimony as well as eating Ruby's delicious home bakes. Jan and Neil were frequent visitors, along with other members of Shirley Evangelical Church, the church where I had committed my life to Christ and which we all now attended.

I was fascinated by one couple from the church, who often came to the farm. Doreen had grown up in Birmingham but had gone to Ecuador as a missionary in the fifties and had lived in the rainforest among one of the indigenous tribes. Out there, she had met and married a young local man called Abdon Villarreal. They knew Jan and Neil very well – in fact, Jan and Neil had once looked after their four children for a few months. While I was at Hill Farm, Doreen and Abdon were on extended home leave and they took an interest in me because they had been in the church the morning I had given my life to Christ. In turn, I loved hearing their stories about their life in Ecuador and the exotic tribal people who live there.

4

God's Special Possession

After a few months at the farm, I found that a profound change had taken place in me. I no longer had any craving for drugs or alcohol, or looked to my old friends for a sense of 'belonging'. I felt a lightness of spirit and had a sense of excitement about what the future might hold. Most surprisingly, I had a passionate desire to tell people about Jesus. However, I'd get frustrated because I didn't know the Bible well and at times I was very hard on myself when old attitudes and reactions came to the surface.

First Peter 2:9 had become the verse I lived by: 'You are a chosen people, a royal priesthood, a holy nation, God's special possession, that you may declare the praises of him who called you out of darkness into his wonderful light.' I took these words as both a promise and a mandate. They summed up all that God had done for me. Being chosen made me special. As one of six children, I had never really felt special – my parents tried hard not to have favourites – but to God I *was* special: chosen, singled out.

Royal and holy? Only God could make someone like me royal – supremely privileged – and holy: clean and pure and set apart for him. Only I knew the depths of my depravity – where I had been and what I had done. I needed that assurance from

God that I was no longer like that in his eyes. I was now one of his own people – he gave me that sense of belonging, security and identity that had been so important to me in my previous life.

And then he had given me a task: I was to declare the praises of him who had called me out of darkness into his wonderful light. I knew exactly what a life spent in darkness was like, and I revelled in the light. My mandate was to tell people what God had done for me and what he could do for them. I felt that it was at the same time both a calling and a commissioning. I had been saved to serve. God had a purpose and a plan for my life.

The leadership at Hill Farm recognized the progress I'd made and began to look for safe ways to begin to reintegrate me into society. My days out with Ruby were one part of the process, but then another opportunity presented itself. I was to spend one day a week at Birmingham Bible Institute, the missionary and ministry training college that Bryan, Carol and Ruby had all gone to. Its founder and principal was the Revd Henry Brash Bonsall, a humble man who lived in close communion with God. He was an amazing man of faith who founded the Institute in 1953 in the firm belief that revival was coming to Britain. He wanted to be ready to teach, equip and commission all those who would be saved, so that they could continue to spread that revival.

Over the years, thousands of students had passed through the ramshackle buildings scattered over a large area of Edgbaston. Many of the Institute's graduates are still serving in tough and inhospitable places on the mission field. Many others are now ministers in churches all over Britain. The Institute's Victorian discipline and the austerity of the conditions there seemed only to enhance the experience of living and working in community, modelling New Testament principles of love, faith, trust, fellowship and prayer. There were no academic requirements for enrolment – the Revd Bonsall believed that God would send those who should study there. Applicants were evaluated at interview on the basis of their call to service and their willingness to live by faith and trust God in every aspect of their lives.

When Bryan asked whether the Institute would allow two residents of Hill Farm to come to lectures one day a week, the Revd Bonsall didn't hesitate to give his approval. It was decided that each Thursday Bob and I would attend three lectures and a pastoral group and would 'pay' for our studies by doing chores at the Institute in the afternoon (as all its students were required to do). I found the first few weeks excruciatingly hard. Neither Bob nor I was used to mixing with other people outside of the farm and we both felt awkward and different. However, the other students treated us kindly and eventually we settled. I enjoyed the lectures enormously and felt I learnt a lot.

In the afternoons I was assigned to help Mrs Bonsall in the kitchen. Her kitchen was legendary! Mrs Bonsall was the most frugal person I'd ever met: twice a week she would go round the markets in Birmingham at the end of the day and pick up whatever vegetables and fruit were unfit for sale. These she would either donate to the Institute or use to feed her family. Sometimes her kitchen itself resembled a market stall, with the floor strewn with decomposing vegetable matter. Whatever efforts I made to clean and tidy were undone within hours.

However, spending time with Mrs Bonsall was a huge blessing. She was quite eccentric – Victorian in both her manner and her dress – but wonderfully kind and generous. She was a devout woman and I noted the way she brought everything to the Lord in prayer. She had an almost childlike faith and trusted God to work out her problems and provide for not only her needs but those of the students. I learnt a lot from her simplicity and her love for everyone, regardless of their background and their lifestyle.

After a year at Hill Farm, I was ready to leave. I felt that the next step for me was to apply to a Bible college. I now knew that God had called me to full-time service of some kind and I needed more teaching and preparation. I wondered whether the Institute would accept a student who was still under the supervision of a probation officer.

I needn't have worried. Mrs Bonsall was my advocate and references from two alumni, Bryan and Ruby, smoothed the way for me to be enrolled for a three-year course. Worcestershire County Council gave me a discretionary grant that would cover all my tuition fees and living expenses and in September 1976 I became one of 150 full-time students of Birmingham Bible Institute (BBI).

Many of my fellow students would later testify at their graduation or at subsequent reunions that their years at BBI were the best of their lives. I certainly enjoyed the fellowship and the lifelong friendships I made there. I enjoyed my studies and the opportunities for evangelism on the streets of Birmingham. I enjoyed speaking at women's fellowship meetings and I enjoyed a trip we did to Rotterdam in the Netherlands to share our faith in the streets using music, drama and mime. However, there were many aspects of college life that I merely endured. Years of loose living made it hard for me to conform to the norms and standards of behaviour that were expected.

At one point, I decided I had had enough of discipline and study and set off to hitchhike to North Wales to join a commune there. I was thumbing a lift on the Hagley Road in Birmingham when a black Morris Minor pulled up. I was just congratulating myself on getting a ride when our college chaplain, the Revd Bob Dunnett, jumped out of the car, along with the head student, Sheila Etherington! One of my fellow students had realized how unhappy I was and had told the college authorities that I was ready to quit.

I knew that I was in big trouble – the terms of my probation meant that I couldn't just leave without telling anyone – so I did what came naturally: I took off! I ran across the busy main road and ducked into a side street to try to evade capture. I vividly remember the sight of the serious Revd Dunnett chasing me in his dog collar and grey raincoat, with Sheila Etherington (nowadays an OBE!) red-faced and breathless in his wake. They eventually caught up with me in a churchyard, where they persuaded me to go back with them and discuss the things that were bothering me.

I have laughed about that episode many times since with friends from those days; but there was another, more serious incident. During my first couple of terms at the Institute, a very nice probation officer had come into college each week to see me, but subsequently I was assigned a new officer and told to report to his office instead. I took a dislike to him and for many weeks I simply failed to show up. A letter was sent to me, with a copy to Hill Farm, warning me that I was breaking the terms of my probation order and would be taken back to court if I failed to make my next appointment.

When the day in question arrived, I decided I would go out to Hill Farm and visit Ruby instead. Her response when she saw me was a shock – I had never seen her angry! Her face went pale, her eyes blazed, her voice trembled and she took hold of me and shook me hard. She couldn't believe that I would ignore the probation order. She was furious that I would risk being sent to prison, and disappointed that my Christian commitment didn't extend to obedience and respect for authority. When I saw her reaction, I was distraught. I was much more concerned about upsetting Ruby than I was about the probation officer! After many tears – on both sides – we rang the probation service to explain that I couldn't attend that day and we made a new appointment.

I did attend that one and met a new probation officer, a Christian who dealt very kindly with me and soon came to the conclusion that, as I was nearing the end of my two-year probation term and was obviously doing well, it was no longer necessary for me to report. Clearly, God had intervened once again on my behalf. I will always be grateful that grace prevailed and I was able to complete my college diploma, with distinction, in 1979.

Over those three years, I was privileged to hear many outstanding Christians who visited the Institute to tell us of the amazing things God was doing around the world. From Cambodia to the Congo, Rwanda to Russia and many other places in between, he was at work and using graduates of BBI to carry out his purposes. Their stories were inspiring, exciting, challenging and faith-building. I wondered whether I would ever be as spiritual as they were, as holy and faith-filled and bold. They were giants of the faith and I was a midget!

From our first day at the Institute, our tutors encouraged us to pray about where God wanted us to serve when we completed our studies and they stressed the need for a 'call'. As the visiting missionaries came each Monday, I listened with excitement to their tales of wild tribesmen, jungle hikes or escape from Russian soldiers. Each week I felt 'called' to a new country, people group or tribe, but within days my 'prayer burden' for it would fade as I heard of something new and more exciting.

In our second year, my good friend Marjorie van Halem and I decided to spend one mealtime a week fasting and praying together about our futures. I had no illusions about being a missionary – I thought I was definitely not holy or spiritual enough, I didn't wear my hair in a bun and I certainly didn't have the right clothes. So, what was I going to do? Marjorie and I made it a priority each week to ask God to show us clearly where he would have us serve.

Doreen and Abdon Villarreal were in Britain during my first two years of college. They lived in a small flat nearby and every week they invited me to tea. It was always a joy to visit them and escape college food. Their home was decorated with colourful Ecuadorian wall hangings and artefacts and I loved eating simple meals of rice and fried eggs with them and listening to their tales of life in the Amazon rainforest.

One story they told me was about a shaman named Samuel who had come to know Jesus as Saviour and Lord and was now an elder in the church. There are two kinds of shaman in Tsachila culture: those known in Spanish as *vegetalistas* or *curanderos*, who know which plants are good for healing, and those known as *tsa ponela* or 'real shamans', who have spent seven years studying their craft under another *tsa pone* – usually their father or an uncle – and have had various artefacts handed down to them. Samuel had been the real deal. For a while after his conversion he had continued to practise as a healer, but in the end he renounced his craft completely, because people were coming to him not just for traditional medicine but for charms and curses. This decision had had a huge impact on his tribe.

The Villarreals gave me a photograph of him on his way to his baptism in the River Cóngoma – he looked magnificent and slightly scary with his head painted red, with bold black stripes on his face and arms, his chest bare and a blue-and-white-striped *manpetsanpa* or woven skirt wrapped around his waist. I tucked the photo inside my Bible, where it reminded me to pray almost every day for Samuel and his family, the fledgling church and those who were coming to Christ.

By my third year, the Villarreals had returned to South America but we kept in contact by post. It took three weeks for a letter to reach Ecuador from Britain. I was now starting to feel anxious about what I would do at the end of my final term. Tentatively I looked into going to Spain with a mission agency I had volunteered with the previous summer, but when that came to nothing I began to panic. What was I to do?

The Villarreals had shared with me their concern that they were getting on in years and had no one younger to help them in their work, but I was anxious that I didn't have a 'call'. I went to talk to one of my tutors. I told her I had an interest in Ecuador, and especially the Tsachila, but felt I wasn't really suited to missionary work. She smiled as I explained my doubts and fears and then advised me to 'push the door'. If God wanted me to go to Ecuador, she said, he would open it.

So, I wrote to Doreen and Abdon and asked them whether they'd ever thought of someone like me joining them in their work in Santo Domingo. Six weeks later, their reply came. My hands shook as I opened the airmail letter, barely glancing at the beautiful stamps on the envelope. The letter was short and it didn't answer my question. Instead, it said simply: 'Go and talk with Auntie Lily at church and tell her what you have asked us.' What kind of a response was that?

Auntie Lily was a godly old woman who had spent most of her life in a wheelchair. She faithfully attended Shirley Evangelical Church and sang loudly and prayed fervently (and loudly). Everyone knew her and every Sunday people would line up to greet her with a kiss. So, the following Sunday I took my place in the line and I told her about my letter from the Villarreals. Her reaction astonished me. 'Praise the Lord!' she shouted. And then she explained: 'The day you gave your heart to Jesus, right here in this church, Doreen asked me to pray for you. She said she believed God would have you in Ecuador with them one day!'

I was astounded. Why would anyone think that a smelly and foul-mouthed biker could become a missionary? Only God could have revealed that to her. I couldn't ask for clearer confirmation: He was calling me to Ecuador. In the days that followed, that became more and more certain as he spoke to me through the Bible. Every day, verses leapt out of the pages at me as God confirmed his plan for me. How true it is that he chooses those who are weak and frail, not the wise or the gifted, to achieve his purposes! He finds the most unlikely people and displays his power through their inadequacies and failings.

So, I was going to be a missionary to Ecuador! I was going to live in the 'jungle' with an 'Indian' tribe! I was going to save the world! But how would I get there? Who would pay my air fare? How would I live? There were so many questions and I had no answers – and no knowledge of how things worked in the mission world. I went to talk to Pastor Bowater. I told him about my call and how it had been confirmed by the Villarreals. I told him they had been praying for me to join them. He replied that he had seen God's work in my life and he believed this was his plan. He told me I could go to Ecuador with the church's blessing. The missionary life is a life of faith, he explained, and so the church would commit to send me just £25 a month. It wasn't enough to live on and I would have to trust God to provide whatever else I needed.

Abdon wrote to tell me that the local Brethren association in Ecuador was willing to help me get a visa. And so it came about that at the age of twenty-four, just a year after I graduated from BBI and five years since I became a Christian, I bought a plane ticket to Miami and from there to Quito.

My church was ecstatic to be sending their very first missionary to the field, but my mother was devastated. My father had passed away two years earlier and my younger sister had since got married and left home. Dad had come to know Jesus as his Saviour just before he died, and Mum had accepted Christ at his funeral; and she had hoped that her only Christian daughter would be around to encourage her and share fellowship with her for many years to come. But now I was leaving her on her own. It would be many years before I came to realize how much my going cost her. It would be many years, too, before she told me she could recognize it was God's will for her and me. For now, all I knew was that I was off on a big adventure with him and nothing was going to hold me back!

5

Oh, I Say! You're *Finally* Here!

The sky was cloudless on that July day in 1980 when an orange Braniff plane landed in Quito with me on board. The 'red-eye special' left Miami daily at 3 a.m. and its passengers could watch the dawn turning the snow-capped Andes pink and red before it made its descent. I was not a seasoned traveller and the journey from London had seemed interminable. It was a relief when the flight attendants finally told us to prepare for landing. Looking out of the window as the plane made its approach, I saw for the first time the almost perfect white cone of the active volcano Cotopaxi. It literally took my breath away. Finally, I had arrived in Ecuador!

Mariscal Sucre is one of the highest international airports in the world, and in 1980 it was still located inside the city. The altitude and the shortness of the runway made landing quite an experience in those days. No sooner had the wheels touched the ground, it seemed, than the pilot put the brakes on hard. The passengers ended up crushed against their seat belts as the plane juddered to a halt.

In those days, long before '9/11', airports were much less security-conscious. At Mariscal Sucre, passengers walked across the tarmac and into the terminal building. Immigration was handled by the police and baggage was unloaded by hand

and left in piles – there were no carousels. I found my two suitcases, allowed a very insistent man to put them on his cart and followed him outside to where the people who had come to meet the plane waited behind a chicken-wire fence. In the rarefied atmosphere at 2,800 metres, I struggled to keep up with my porter as I tried to spot a friendly face behind the wire.

Eventually, I heard rather than saw Doreen Villarreal. 'Oh, I say! *Me muero*, you're *finally* here!' In spite of her thirty-five or more years in Ecuador, she had lost nothing of her British accent and manner – although she often mixed them with Spanish. I was so glad to see her and Abdon and to be enveloped in their hugs! They steered me and the porter to a white Ford pick-up and we loaded my cases into the back. Then the three of us squeezed into the cab and we set off for the guest-house where they had stayed the previous night.

After breakfast – my second of the day – we discussed our plans. The question was: how tired was I? If I wasn't too bad, they said, we could head straight on to Santo Domingo de los Colorados, but otherwise we could wait until the next day. The truth was that the adrenalin had long ago kicked in at the sheer excitement of finally being on Ecuadorian soil, so I was more than ready for the adventure to continue. The drive down to Santo Domingo was something like 150 kilometres (just under 100 miles), but on tortuous mountain roads. I took a shower and had a short rest and then we set off. We'd decided to buy some food before we left Quito for a picnic en route, but imagine my surprise when we pulled up at a Kentucky Fried Chicken! At that time, it was the only fast-food restaurant in the country and a KFC takeaway was considered a luxury, but it was hardly what I'd been expecting.

The road from Quito down to Santo Domingo was – and to some extent still is – the most spectacular and most terrifying in the world. Heading south out of the capital, it joins the Pan-American Highway for about 50 kilometres and then turns west towards the Pacific coast. Within the space of another 50 kilometres, it drops from over 3,000 metres to 1,000 through a series of hairpin bends. The road had only two lanes in those days and the surface was poor, and in the afternoons it was often enveloped in thick fog that reduced visibility to just a few metres. The greatest hazard, however, was other vehicles, and particularly the buses and lorries that would hurtle down the road, passing each other on blind bends, often at great speed. Not surprisingly, there have been many hundreds of deaths, if not thousands, over the years I have travelled that road since then. I have been in a couple of accidents myself, thankfully minor in terms of the injuries but major in terms of the damage to the vehicles.

The scenery on that road is breathtaking. High sierra, or *páramo*, gives way to dense cloud forest on the descent. Waterfalls tumble down the mountainsides, sometimes onto the road. Wild orchids spring out of the lush vegetation, and flocks of brightly coloured parrots squawk overhead. It is truly a white-knuckle ride in every sense!

Between Quito and Santo Domingo, there were only three small settlements. Aloag is really a truck stop, even today: the road is lined with shacks where 'handymen' work with big hammers and a few other tools to 'fix' cars and repair the heavy goods vehicles that carry freight between Quito and the port cities of Guayaquil, Esmeraldas and Manta. The other two are Tandapi and Alluriquin and their only distinction is that they are, respectively, one hour and twenty minutes from Santo Domingo! Many times in the years to come I would be filled with joy and relief at seeing the lights of one of these settlements after long hours stuck behind heavy lorries as they wound their way painfully down the mountainside in thick fog. Often, I would be simply too afraid to attempt to pass them. The bumpers of some of the trucks had stark reminders painted on them: *Si no vuelvo es que he ido a Dios* ('If I don't come back, it's because I've gone to God'). Others bore less sobering but funnier messages that entertained me as I followed them on their laborious way, such as *Trabaja no envidia* ('Work! Don't envy me!').

On that first day, however, I was an innocent adventurer and oblivious to the dangers of that mountain road. I exclaimed delightedly at the waterfalls, 'ooh'ed and 'aah'ed at the orchids and marvelled at the lushness of the vegetation. As we neared our destination, the air became hot and muggy as we entered the subtropics. Eventually the tarmac road gave way to gravel as we arrived in Santo Domingo. Here, the streets were lined with wooden buildings and teemed with people. Santo Domingo has always been a commercial hub and a hive of activity, as it is a natural waypoint between the sierra and the coast. Today, it is still one of the fastest-growing cities in Ecuador.

We turned in through some gates into a beautiful compound with green lawns on either side of a short driveway. Along one side of the property there were palms and what looked like citrus trees. On the other side, flowering plants added a bright splash of colour to the grass – I recognized busy Lizzies, geraniums and huge red hibiscus. Straight ahead of us, at the end of the drive, was what looked like a chicken coop. 'Here we are!' trilled Doreen in a voice like Joyce Grenfell.

I almost asked where the house was and I'm so glad I didn't – the 'chicken coop' was it! I'm not sure what I'd been expecting but it wasn't a small wooden shack, half-eaten by termites, with wire mesh in the window frames instead of glass. Doreen ushered me in through the door and at once I could see that she had made it a real home. It was spotlessly clean (except for the piles of termite droppings, which were no sooner dusted away than more appeared!) with a comfortable sofa, chairs with embroidered covers and cushions, lino on the floor and potted plants and flowers. My small room had a single bed with a patchwork cover, a bedside table, a lamp, a chest of drawers and a curtain to hang my clothes behind. I soon felt at home. We ate a light meal and I marvelled at how quickly night fell at the equator, with almost no twilight. I fell asleep to the strange but soothing sounds of the rainforest.

The first morning I woke up in Ecuador was characterized by the unfamiliar hubbub of a rural community in the subtropics: cocks crowing, hens clucking, dogs barking, birds singing, people shouting, children crying. So very different from what I had known in England!

I quickly learnt that I was something of a spectacle for the local folk. There were few tourists in those days, even in Quito, and those who did venture south of the equator tended to visit the Galapagos Islands and the expensive lodges in Amazonia. They would stay in smart hotels in the capital and then hightail it back to the United States or Europe, without ever venturing into the real Ecuador or even talking to a real Ecuadorian. Apart from the missionaries in Santo Domingo – now seven of us in all – there were just a few North Americans in town, generally working on agricultural projects for the Peace Corps. So, when a new foreigner arrived in the community it was customary to pay a visit, usually with any of your children who were studying *Ingles* in school so that they could get in some practice! Unlike my colleagues, I couldn't speak a word of Spanish at this point, so conversation was very limited and involved a lot of hand signals and giggling.

It was very soon apparent that I was going to have to learn Spanish, and quickly! This caused me a fair bit of anxiety – as a schoolgirl, my flair for foreign languages had proved to be non-existent. After five painful years of learning French vocabulary lists and trying to conjugate verbs, my teacher had decided I would *not* be entered for the O-level exam but instead should attempt the CSE, which was not really worth much unless you got a grade 1! She further boosted my confidence by remarking that I was the first pupil in the entire history of Tudor Grange Grammar School for Girls who'd been entered for a CSE in French!

I've often thought since that actually what I found hard was not the language itself but the way it was taught. In truth, I have an ear for accents and I'm able to mimic people easily, so the way I ended up learning Spanish was just to copy what other people said. Many times I would come out with a whole sentence to the astonishment of my colleagues, who would say, 'What does *that* mean?' To which I would reply: 'I'm not sure, but I know it's what you say if you want to buy a bottle of Coke.'

There was a Scottish missionary about my age, called Jane Wyllie, who had arrived in Santo Domingo six months before me and within a few days she came to the house to make my acquaintance. We went into town together to drink Coke and eat cake, but our conversation was awkward. I think we were tiptoeing around each other, trying to size each other up. A few days later, she invited me over for a meal. She was house-sitting for another British missionary who had gone home 'on furlough' (when missionaries report back to the churches that sponsor them and raise funds for themselves and their work).

The evening turned out to be memorable in several ways. I can't remember what was on the menu except that one of

the items was best described as tasteless green slime. I strug-
gled to swallow it and then struggled further to keep it down.
'Sorry about the lettuce,' said Jane. 'I boiled it so it wouldn't
upset your stomach.' So that's what it was! Like a true Brit,
I replied, 'Oh, it's fine. It's quite nice, really.' Then we both
burst out laughing. The ice was broken! Later that evening, as
Jane walked me home, we saw that a fair had come to town.
Hesitantly, she told me how much she loved riding the big
Ferris wheel . . . 'Me, too!' I exclaimed and before long the
two of us were riding high above the city, laughing and eating
candy floss and celebrating the start of what was to prove a
wonderful, solid, fun-filled friendship.

The day after my arrival in Santo Domingo, we were due
to pay a visit to one of the Tsachila communities. I was beside
myself with excitement. Finally, I would meet face-to-face the
people I had been praying for for years! I longed to see them,
to be among them and get to know them. That had been the
desire of my heart ever since I first knew God had called me to
this ethnic group.

The Tsachila are also known as 'Colorado Indians'. The
mestizo people of Spanish descent called them *colorado* (which
means 'reddish-coloured') on account of their custom of using
the bright vermillion dye they get from the seed pods of the
achiote bush on their hair and skin. Their own name for
themselves in their Tsafiki language means 'real people' or 'true
people'. Today they have abandoned the practice of dyeing
their skin but the men continue to shave their heads below the
tops of their ears and then plaster their hair with achiote seeds
mixed with Vaseline and shape it like a smooth inverted bowl
or visor.

Missionary work among the Tsachila had begun in the 1950s
and Doreen was one of the pioneers. Elisabeth Elliot, whose

husband Jim was later martyred in the eastern rainforests of Ecuador by the Waorani (the tribe known pejoratively by their Quichua neighbours as the Auca, or 'savages'), had also spent time with the Tsachila and had done some basic linguistic work with them. By the time I arrived on the scene, there were two couples involved in the ministry: Doreen and Abdon Villarreal and Bruce and Joyce Moore, a couple from the United States who had not only written the language down but then spent twenty-five years translating the New Testament into Tsafiki so the Tsachila would have the word of God in their own tongue.

My first encounter with the 'true people' was exactly what I thought a trip into the 'jungle' would be like. It lived up to all my expectations, and actually exceeded some of them! We set out from Santo Domingo in the pick-up around two o'clock in the afternoon. Doreen was wearing the home-woven striped wraparound skirt the indigenous women wear every day, while Abdon had wellington boots on and carried a net bag with a few books in it and a large machete, which he placed carefully on the floor of the cab. We drove along a reasonable tarmac road for 26 kilometres or so and then turned off onto a dirt track.

As we bounced our way over the potholes, clouds of dust rose up and we had to close all the windows. I was soon sweating profusely! After about an hour of driving on a steadily deteriorating surface, through small streams and over 'bridges' that were essentially two logs over a gully, we came to a large, swift-flowing river and came to a halt. We had arrived. Well, we had arrived as far as the pick-up would take us and from this point on we would walk.

The first problem was how to cross the river. The Pupusá is not a great torrent in the dry season but still it is about 20 metres wide, with a rocky bed, and can be quite deep in the middle. It seemed we had two options: wading across, which of course would mean getting our feet wet at the very least, or trying to walk over on a felled tree trunk that spanned the river like a bridge. No attempt had been made to flatten the curve of the trunk, let alone provide any kind of handrail, and it looked very risky to me.

Doreen opted for wading, while Abdon decided to try the 'bridge'. After I'd watched him all but skip across without even a wobble, I decided to follow his example. It hadn't occurred to me that a lifetime of living in the rainforest had given Abdon much better balance, even in his fifties, than I would ever have. Not only did I wobble, I almost fell in. Abdon instantly jumped into the river and waded over so that he could hold my hand and hold me steady. It wouldn't be the last time I would be grateful for his upbringing! He later proved to be an amazing killer of snakes, chaser of anteaters, catcher of fish, builder of rafts and a thousand other things.

Once we had all reached dry land, we started our hike. In fact we were in secondary forest, but to my inexperienced eyes it was 'deep jungle'. I was exhilarated to be in Amazonia, surrounded (or so I imagined) by deadly snakes, wild animals and fierce tribesmen. Of course, the reality was that, yes, I was in subtropical rainforest and, yes, there were almost certainly venomous snakes nearby, and maybe some other animals, mostly harmless. The Tsachila were the only tribespeople around and no one has ever described them as 'fierce'. I would later learn how gentle, kind and shy these red-painted people are, but at that moment I felt like a true pioneer.

The Tsachila are agriculturalists who grow, hunt or catch all they need to live. Their staple food is plantain, boiled and mashed and shaped into a fat sausage, which they eat with soup, meat or fish. The word for 'plantain' is *anó* and the word for 'food' is *anó-ila*, which shows just how essential this green banana is to their diet. They do also grow cash crops that they sell in the markets in Santo Domingo, and so as we hiked through the forest we eventually came to some of their coffee and cocoa plantations.

The afternoon was very hot and humid and after an hour of trudging up and down hills and pushing my way through thick vegetation, the excitement of being a pioneer was beginning to fade. Sweat bees were buzzing around my face and little black flies were biting my legs and arms, and the six-hour time difference between Britain and Ecuador was taking its toll. Were we nearly there? Was there even a 'there' to be? Not wanting to be a complainer at this early stage of my missionary career, I refrained from asking, but after yet one more stumble over an exposed root I almost spoke out. At that very moment, a man stepped out of the forest right into our path.

My first thought was that this was the strangest person I had ever seen. He was a few inches taller than me and my eyes were drawn to two things: his bright red 'helmet' of hair and the large jungle knife in his hand. Wow! I suddenly realized I was looking at my very first 'Colorado Indian'. A real, live Tsachi! He looked amazing. His face and arms were painted with black stripes and his lips and fingers were dyed completely black. He was bare-chested and had a number of brightly coloured scarves knotted around his neck. He also wore a pair of nice, neat trousers which were tucked into rubber boots.

Abdon and Doreen greeted him warmly. This was Augustine and he was going to guide us the rest of the way to his community. I was introduced and managed to use all the Tsafiki words I had learnt: *Senan joyun?* ('Are you well?'). *Senan joyoe* ('I am well'). Augustine was greatly amused. After that, in the company of our colourful friend and Christian brother, the rest of the journey to our destination didn't seem so dreary. Augustine, like many of his people, had a soft voice and a gentle manner. I felt thrilled and incredibly privileged to be going into his community, to see at first-hand what their lives were like. Little did I know that for a few months his home would become my home and I would live as part of the family, with him, his wife and their two daughters, as I tried to learn the Tsafiki tongue.

6

Baby Talk

Santo Domingo was not a bad place to live in the 1980s. The streets were just gravel, the electricity was sporadic, drinking water was unheard of and personal safety was always an issue, and yet the friendliness and hospitality of the locals, the lush, green surroundings (with clean rivers to bathe in) and the delicious food from the coast made up for all these shortcomings.

My days soon fell into a routine. I got up at first light, which came at 6 a.m. every day (being on the equator, Ecuador has twelve hours of daylight and twelve of darkness all year round). I had breakfast with Doreen and Abdon, during which we would listen to *Himnos de la Vida Cristiana* ('Hymns of the Christian Life'), broadcast by HCJB's powerful transmitter in Quito. Then I would take a couple of Spanish grammar books and go and sit quietly in the half-built shell that was eventually to become the Villarreals' new home. As missionaries living by faith, they were depending on God for the funds to enable them to move out of the 'chicken coop' into something more substantial.

Doreen and Abdon had spent many years living and farming in the rainforest near one of the Tsachila communities. When their children needed more schooling than Doreen could provide, the whole family moved into Santo Domingo, where they bought a large piece of land on the edge of the city. They continued their ministry to the Tsachila by travelling out to their communities and also received folk who would stop by their house for food, medicine, advice or just a chat when they came to town.

Next to the house there was an even smaller building that served as a clinic – Doreen had had some basic training as a nurse's aide in the 1950s at the grandly named Missionary School of Medicine in London – and another room for guests. In those days, transport to the nearby forest areas where the Tsachila lived was sporadic and unreliable and often people needed a place to stay over if they missed the last truck out. The Tsachila have little need of the kind of comforts I was accustomed to and some straw mats and a blanket on the wooden floor were considered sufficient for a good night's sleep.

The Villarreal's house was in a very strategic position and on most days there was a steady stream of visitors. The Tsachila are very shy people, so it was usual for one family group to hang around the gate waiting until the previous group had left. Sometimes there were several groups 'in line' waiting, such was the power of their culture of avoidance. They even have a word for this, *lu*, which refers to their natural embarrassment and timidity with each other. In times past, it was common for whole conversations to take place without any eye contact – and even with one party squatting with their backs to the other!

I was desperate to learn Tsafiki so that I could talk with these beautiful, colourful, mysterious, gentle people. I learnt to count in their language and, like a child, I learnt my colours, and I tried to pick up a few phrases; but Doreen was adamant that first I must learn Spanish and only then would I be allowed to start studying Tsafiki. There was a rule she enforced strictly in the house: when anyone was present who didn't speak English, only Spanish must be spoken. Abdon had spent a lot of time in Britain and his English was good, but there was a young student called Joni who helped Doreen in the house and to begin with I had to spend lunchtimes in silence because I couldn't converse *en español!*

Looking back, I'm grateful to Doreen for insisting that I learn Spanish and learn it well. It's now been my language for thirty-five years and I'm glad I can engage at every level in Latin-American society. I even did research for an MSc gathering data from interviews conducted in Spanish. At the time, however, learning it was an excruciating experience for me. I'm naturally gregarious and chatty and it seemed to me that my personality was being squashed as I struggled to connect and communicate with the people I met each day. At times, I became despondent. 'I'm funny,' I'd complain to Jane. 'People laugh at my jokes in English. I love to talk, but here I'm like an idiot, just using baby words and smiling.' Jane was further ahead of me in learning Spanish – she had spent six months at language school in Quito – but her strong Scottish accent affected her pronunciation. People found her charming to listen to but very hard to understand.

Each weekday afternoon, I would head into town to try out on some unsuspecting shopkeepers the vocabulary I had learnt that morning. I was one of the few foreigners around and they soon got to know me and became used to me asking for 'Ten Thursdays, please.' Smiling, they would hand over ten eggs – *jueves* and *huevos* sounded the same to my untrained ear. Thankfully, Ecuadorians are very gracious towards foreigners and will try their hardest to understand their mangled and mispronounced Spanish.

Jane and I often met up in town to share a Coke together. It was always a relief to be able to relate to someone on an adult level from a similar cultural background. She had been raised in a strong Christian family and had an unshakeable faith in God and a deep understanding of the Scriptures. She was a gifted Bible teacher and I learnt many deep spiritual truths from her. She was also beautiful, with the deepest-blue eyes and palest skin I have ever seen. Ecuadorian men would stare in admiration as she walked through the city, often calling out to her: '*Guapa!* Hey, gorgeous!' She had a wonderful sense of humour and an infectious laugh and many times we would be doubled up as we recounted our mistakes and misunderstandings in the Spanish language. We compared notes and I believe we kept each other sane!

Both of us had a passionate desire to share the gospel of Jesus with the Ecuadorian people. In our youth and inexperience there was probably an arrogance, too. It was as if we were saying to God, 'OK, Lord, you can relax now. Ecuador is safe now we're here!' Our bumptious attitude must have irritated our older, more seasoned colleagues, but they were kind to us and tolerated it.

Sunday was market day in Santo Domingo and the streets bustled with country folk bringing in their produce to sell. Great 'heads' of green bananas and huge sacks of coffee and cocoa beans were hauled into town, and people waited patiently in line in the hot sun to get them weighed, while others haggled with the merchants over prices. Finally, cash in hand, they would head to the markets to buy kerosene, candles, matches and salt to take back to their homes in the forest. The Tsachila were there as well. The women could be seen standing in groups in the street, dressed in their brightly coloured skirts or *tunans*, waiting for their menfolk to return with the proceeds of their sales so that they, too, could go to the markets to buy beads and ribbons, machetes and knives.

Each Sunday, Tsachila from the different communities would crowd into a wooden building on the Villarreals' property for a service – I noticed that they seemed to lose some of their shyness when they came to Christ. Sitting on balsawood benches known as *chipolos*, they would sing the few songs they had in Tsafiki, with many repetitions so that the women (who were mostly illiterate) could learn the words. Someone would read some portions of Scripture from the parts of the New Testament that Bruce had translated into Tsafiki, and then either he or Abdon would give a simple message.

We also took communion. I still marvel that, wherever I go on the planet, people who know and love the Lord Jesus break bread with each other. This simple act overcomes all barriers of ethnicity and language and creates such a bond between believers! The type of bread and wine varies from country to country, culture to culture, but the focus on Jesus and his love for humankind, his death on the cross and his resurrection is the same worldwide.

Sunday was always a busy day. Often, many Tsachila would stay behind after church to seek Doreen's advice on a medical matter or ask Abdon for help in making a deposit in the bank, getting a new identity card or registering a newborn baby in the civil registry in town. Some of the men could speak a little Spanish but generally they needed Abdon as an intermediary between their world and the Spanish-speaking one. Few of them who were over twenty or so could read – and none of the women over sixteen. In addition, they had to deal with the prejudice of the *mestizos* toward the indigenous. Sometimes they were treated like pets rather than human beings or, worse, they were exploited and cheated. Much of Abdon's work was advocacy on their behalf.

We took Mondays as our day off, and on these days I was especially grateful for Jane's friendship and company. There was not a lot to do around Santo Domingo. Sometimes we would all go to one of the rivers near the city to swim and have a picnic. The coolness of the water always provided welcome relief from the heat and the humidity, and the relative silence and stillness of the rainforest calmed my soul. The lush vegetation, beautiful flowers and colourful birds, not to mention the warm, moist smell, Jane and I agreed, were soothing to brains that were frazzled by learning Spanish.

Abdon liked to take a fishing net along on these trips. This circular *atarraya* was about 2 metres in diameter, hand-woven out of forest vines and weighted around the edge with small pieces of lead. He had learnt the art of fishing with it as a young boy. He would stand in the river or perch on a rock with the net draped over his arm, with one of the pieces of lead in his mouth. He would then cast the net in such a way that it opened out as it hit the water and trapped the fish beneath it – he had to be careful to release the lead from his mouth at exactly the right moment. Abdon was very proficient at this and sometimes we would feast on delicious fish, barbecued at the riverside, with green bananas. Those were special days!

Jane and I shared an adventurous streak, but the Villarreals felt a need to shelter these two young women so far from home and at times we felt stifled. One Monday, we decided to take a ninety-minute ride to Quevedo, the nearest large town to Santo Domingo, even though neither of us was proficient in Spanish. At first the rickety bus we boarded was fairly empty, but as it crawled on its way it stopped frequently to pick people up: people carrying chickens, people carrying pigs, people carrying huge machetes, people carrying sacks of corn or oranges, heads of bananas, pineapples – in fact, all kinds of everything!

When the bus was full, they continued to pile in or even climbed on top of it. At one point, a man launched himself across our laps, threw open the window and climbed out of the bus just in time to save a pig in a sack from falling off the roof! Our initial shock quickly turned to laughter and we spent the next five minutes trying to suppress our mirth as the pig was returned to its place and tied securely and the owner got back into the bus by the same route he had left it.

Once we had got over this bizarre interruption, our conversation turned to more serious matters. What was the spiritual state of these people? Had they heard about Jesus? If not, who would tell them? Most Ecuadorians are nominally Catholic and out in the countryside in those days everyone lived in fear of the priest, though their 'faith' seemed more like a mix of traditional animistic beliefs with just a veneer of Catholicism. Most people attended Mass occasionally, got their babies baptized and loosely followed the teachings of the church, but they lived in fear of evil spirits, believed that many illnesses were caused by 'bad air' or 'the evil eye' and went to the shaman when they were sick.

Jane and I agreed that God had sent us to Ecuador as missionaries to proclaim the good news of the forgiveness of sin that was made possible by Jesus' sacrificial death. We decided then and there that we had a responsibility to tell all the people on the bus about this. Jane went first. Fighting her way to the middle of the bus so she could be heard better, she raised her voice and started to give a clear and simple presentation of the gospel.

Her Spanish was very imperfect but the effect it had on the other passengers was electric. Everyone stopped talking. People turned and craned their necks to see who was speaking. They paid attention to her every word. Clearly, the anointing of the

Holy Spirit was on Jane that day! She delivered a powerful message of love and grace and forgiveness and hope and, when she had finished, she took her seat to loud applause. I got up to hand out gospel tracts and everybody wanted one.

We pulled into the bus station at Quevedo and people shook hands with us as they got off and thanked us for our message. We were thrilled to have had the opportunity to share the gospel with so many. Finally, we thought, we're *real* missionaries!

On the journey back that afternoon, it was my turn to speak. I still hadn't mastered the past tenses in Spanish, so I prayed that my brief testimony and presentation of the gospel would be accepted by God and that his Holy Spirit would make sense of it to my audience. Certainly, people didn't seem too puzzled by the fact that I told my story entirely in the present tense, pointing back over my shoulder to indicate that something was now behind me. And when I had finished, I, too, received appreciative applause.

Doreen and Abdon listened in amused surprise as we told them of our adventures, and thereafter they began to be less protective as they realized that we were starting to feel more confident and at home in our adopted country. 'Mondays in Quevedo' became a regular part of our week and we went on to preach not only on the buses but in the marketplace and town square as well. Such was our enthusiasm to share Christ with the people of Ecuador.

Finally the day came when my Spanish was considered good enough for me to be allowed to tackle another language: Tsafiki, which means 'true words'. Unlike Spanish, there are no 'Teach yourself Tsafiki' books and the only people then who could speak it apart from the three thousand or so Tsachila were the Villarreals and the Moores. Bruce was the expert, having written the language down and spent twenty-five years translating the New Testament – indeed, the Tsachila often said, quite seriously, that he spoke Tsafiki better than they did!

I knew that my learning style was better suited to listening and imitating rather than struggling to master vocabulary and grammar, so I decided the best approach would be total immersion. Accordingly, with a sleeping bag and a few other basic belongings, I set off to go and live with Augustine's family in the Naranjo community. This is one of the smaller and more isolated communities, and the only one that didn't have a school. There was no road to it. Augustine and his wife, Luz Maria, and their two girls were the only baptized believers in Naranjo. Very few of the people there spoke Spanish – Augustine was the only member of his family that spoke any at all – so there would be little opportunity for me to 'cheat' by lapsing into that. My future ministry depended on me learning Tsafiki and Naranjo seemed like an ideal place to do so.

Living with Augustine and his family taught me a lot about what life is like for the Tsachila. His house was made from split bamboo and stood on stilts, surrounded by the forest. It had a tin roof, which kept the rain off effectively but turned the interior into a sauna in the heat of the day and prevented any conversation during the daily downpours in the wet season. I came to love hearing the roar of the rain approaching through the forest and making a mad dash to reach shelter before the first drops reached us. On occasions, I would stay outside with Augustine's two girls, enjoying a shower fully clothed under the water pouring off the roof.

The house was divided into two parts. The main living area had half-height walls and was light and airy. The other part was fully enclosed and all five of us slept there together. I soon got used to this. We lay on rush mats on the wooden floor, but I had a pillow, for which I was grateful, and I curled up under a sheet, with my sleeping bag underneath me for a bit of extra padding.

Our diet was simple: green bananas three times a day, boiled and mashed and rolled into sausages, accompanied by fish, eggs or (on special occasions) the meat of a wild boar, agouti or armadillo that Augustine had killed in the forest.

I wanted to make myself useful, so we decided I should teach basic literacy. Augustine, Luz Maria and the two girls were all keen to learn to read. Bruce and his indigenous assistants had recently completed the translation of the New Testament into Tsafiki and everyone was eager to learn to understand 'God's New Carvings' for themselves. As I prepared my classes, however, I soon realized that there were obstacles to be overcome. First, there were no textbooks or basic reading books, so Bruce and Joyce started helping me to make 'primers' and flash cards. Tsafiki is based on a pattern of vowel–consonant–vowel (with the occasional diphthong thrown in), which means that if someone can learn all the individual sounds they should be able to work out how each written word is pronounced. It all seemed so simple in theory.

In practice, it was anything but. I very quickly established that I am not a gifted teacher, not least because I lack one essential qualification: patience. 'How hard can this be?' I would ask myself as one of my students struggled to read out *Mama te cae* ('Grandma gets firewood'). Thirty seconds earlier, she'd seemingly been able to read it perfectly! My months of teaching in Naranjo were excruciating, though I did find that the children, who turned up most mornings if there was nothing more exciting going on, learnt more quickly than the adults and it was gratifying to see their progress.

Each afternoon, I would try to help with the chores around the farm, harvesting coffee and cocoa beans and plantains. My admiration for the Tsachila grew. Their lives are tough and they have to work hard simply to survive, sowing and harvesting and keeping the rainforest at bay. They spend hours hacking it back with huge machetes to stop it encroaching on their crops and their living space. Even their leisure time is spent looking for food. Hunting and fishing expeditions are exciting events but often involve walking many kilometres through the forest loaded down with fishing nets, machetes, bananas and cooking pots.

The Tsachila are expert at fishing with the *atarraya*. They also use a root from a forest plant called 'barbasco', which they pound against a rock in the river until it gives out a milky juice. This seems somehow to remove the oxygen from the water, so that the fish come to the surface, gasping for air, and are easily caught. Barbasco fishing has been banned in Ecuador now (because it kills even the fish too small to eat, and also contaminates the water), but the community still love to recall the fun we used to have and the feasts we shared on the river-bank after the women had cooked the day's catch.

While I was working and fishing alongside the Tsachila, I came to realize how useless I was to them. What did I have to offer, after all? I had come to Ecuador with a somewhat arrogant attitude that I 'was needed', but it was clear that this wasn't the case. My studies and my preparation for mission counted for very little. I couldn't carry a whole head of bananas – it was too heavy for me. I was very slow at picking coffee and the insects crawling up my arms and biting my legs distracted me so much that usually the fruit of my afternoon's labour was pathetic. When I dived under the water in search of the armour-plated catfish that clung to the underside of rocks, I could at best catch one. My Tsachila friends would surface after many minutes underwater with one in each hand and one in their mouth!

I began to ask myself: How can I be more use? Why had God brought me to Ecuador if I had nothing to give? Teaching people to read was helpful but I could see I was not very good at it. Finally, it dawned on me that God's purpose was to do something in *me*. Recognizing my own inadequacy was the start. Self-confidence and self-sufficiency are not what he required. Rather, he wanted me to put all my trust in him, not in myself and my own abilities. He wanted to work through me, and in that way he was able to achieve far more than I could ever imagine. It was a good lesson for life.

My language skills were improving and I could hold simple conversations, but I was feeling isolated living in such a remote place. We went into Santo Domingo only once every two weeks for church. On those occasions I suffered sensory overload – the noise, the traffic and the crowds were overwhelming – but once we returned to our home in the forest I realized how lonely I was. How much I missed Jane and my other friends in the city! How much I wanted to talk about something other than bananas, the neighbours' pigs or the price of coffee beans!

After six months with Augustine and his family, I moved to Cóngoma, a larger community which was more accessible by road and had many more believers. There, I had my own house, a wooden structure with a tin roof. I still had no electricity or running water, but I was happy to have some privacy and I still had good neighbours.

7

I Don't Need Preaching, I Need Food

The community of Cóngoma Grande is named after the River Cóngoma that runs through it. Back in the 1980s, a gravel road snaked down to it from the main road out of Santo Domingo and in the rainy season this would deteriorate to a mud track pockmarked with huge potholes every few metres. Travelling the last 10 kilometres to Cóngoma was a bone-jarring experience that took well over an hour.

Still, those conditions were a distinct improvement on those that Bruce and Joyce and their family had endured in the fifties when the journey from Santo Domingo took a full day on horseback. Each month, they would buy supplies in town and load them onto mules, which they had to pull, push and otherwise cajole along the muddy trails to the community they called 'home'.

The Moores were linguists who had gone to Ecuador to write the Tsafiki language down and then make a translation of the New Testament. However, much of their time initially was taken up with learning to live in the rainforest without any modern amenities. Every meal had to be prepared from scratch and cooked over a wood fire; every drop of water for drinking, washing or bathing had to be fetched from the river. Bruce burnt a lot of 'midnight oil' working on linguistics once darkness had fallen and their four children (and the early-to-bed Tsachila) were asleep. It was a great day in July 1980 when 'God's New Carvings' (the New Testament in Tsafiki) was completed, printed, dedicated and placed into the hands of the people.

I was blessed to have Bruce's assistance in learning the language. For about a year, he spent time helping me to master its very complex grammar. He and Joyce knew they would soon be leaving Ecuador and they felt that this investment of his time in teaching me was worthwhile.

Life in Cóngoma was fun. It was a larger community than Naranjo, and closer-knit. There were other houses near to mine and people walking past my door often stopped to pay a visit. One event not to be missed was the 'show' when I removed my contact lenses. The Tsachila were fascinated that I was able to do this – to them it was completely mind-boggling – and once they found out that I took them out every night, word went around so that others could come and watch. Eventually, I had to exclude spectators altogether, as the press of people peering into my eyes and their hilarious running commentary were so off-putting that I wasn't able to remove my lenses easily and safely.

I felt very much at home in the community, relaxed and safe. My neighbours kept a close eye on me, dealing with any snakes that ventured onto my patio and generously sharing with me the fish they caught and the meat they hunted. They seemed to feel they had a responsibility to keep me alive. However, while I was touched by their kindness, it also bothered me. I would reflect endlessly on my limitations and my dependence on the Tsachila. It seemed that things were back to front: they had no need of me whatsoever, but I could not survive without them! I wanted to be useful to them, I wanted to serve them,

I wanted to *do* something for them – but what? The only gifts I had that were useful to them were that I could speak Spanish and I could read.

The early eighties were a time of unprecedented growth in the Tsachila church. Once the New Testament got into the hands of the believers, it aroused huge interest among the other Tsachila. This was the very first real book in Tsafiki and everyone wanted to read it. Many Tsachila had attended basic school at least but had learnt to read in Spanish. They could make out the words on the page, but the meaning of those words was often not clear to them. It was amazing to hear them 'sounding out' the words in 'God's New Carvings' and watch the smiles spread across their faces as they actually understood their meaning. 'God speaks to me in Tsafiki!' many would exclaim. Never before had a book spoken to them in their own language. This seemed to open their minds and hearts to the Spirit of God and as a result many dedicated their lives to Christ.

The community had no church building and so each Friday night the believers would meet in someone's house to sing, read from the New Testament, discuss what they had read and pray together. Different families took it in turns to host these gatherings and invite their unsaved neighbours. Their faith was very straightforward. If 'God's carvings' said it, they believed it. Many times, simple prayers of faith were offered for the sick and they were instantly healed. No one considered this unusual, or even miraculous – didn't God's word clearly tell us to pray for the sick so that they would be healed? It was refreshing to be part of such a theologically uncomplicated group.

Almost every week, someone who was attending for the first time would stand up, all their shyness apparently forgotten, and announce that they had 'let Jesus get them', as they put it. The spread of the gospel and the growth of the church were astonishing. A lively group formed of young people who were truly on fire for God. They testified bravely to some of the shamans and elders, the hardened sceptics of the tribe, telling them of their need to repent of their sins and 'let Jesus get them'. They readily made the journey to take the good news of Jesus Christ to other Tsachila communities.

On one of these occasions, a group of young people was travelling to a neighbouring community, riding on the hardy little horses the Tsachila use. I accompanied them, along with Abdon and Aurelio, one of the older men in the church. I had a rather larger, fancier mount, named Roobarb (because she had been bought for me, from a breeder in Santo Domingo, by Ruby and another friend from England called Barbara). After a while, the young people decided to let their horses race and we set off at an alarming pace. I was never a great horsewoman and I clung on to Roobarb's mane as she galloped through the forest. Suddenly, frightened by some wild boar that were foraging beside the trail, she reared. I hit the ground – hard!

I came around to the sun shining in my eyes and the sound of sobbing. '*Puyaca joe!* She is dead!' I squinted in the light to see several red heads bent over me, faces streaked with tears. I tried to move, but the pain was unbearable. Abdon appeared and after a few minutes he helped me to get up. There was nothing else for it but to remount and head back home. Every bone in my body felt bruised and disjointed as we proceeded at a walk. Back at the house, two of my neighbours, Arturo and Chinche, took Roobarb to rub her down and feed and water her while I fell onto my bed. The next day, I was unable to move. In fact, it was several days before I could walk unaided. I never again allowed my horse to do more than a trot.

I continued to give reading classes in both Cóngoma and Naranjo. I think it made me feel useful. Once a week, I travelled on horseback to Augustine's house, which took about two hours each way. I enjoyed those trips, swaying slowly through the forest lost in thought as Roobarb picked her way along, stepping over fallen trees, wading through streams and rivers, straining up muddy hills and slipping down the other side. As I said, I am no horsewoman, so I was content to hang on to the reins – and sometimes her mane as well – and let Roobarb find her own way.

One day as I was riding to Naranjo, I noticed a man approaching on the trail ahead. He was dressed in work clothes and carried a large machete. I suddenly realized how isolated I was out there. I hadn't seen a house or even another person for a good forty minutes. 'Who is this man?' I wondered. 'Why is he out here, so far from anywhere? Am I safe?' I'd heard stories of women being attacked in the forest by the infamous *Manabas* (that is, men from the province of Manabi). To be fair, my experiences of these men so far had been good – I'd often hitched a ride in a truck heading into town with a friendly *Manaba* at the wheel – but at that moment I could only doubt the wisdom of travelling such remote trails alone and wonder how fast Roobarb could run – and whether I would manage to stay on.

The man drew near and greeted me: '*Buenos dias.*' (Ecuadorians are extremely polite to strangers.) I returned his greeting. 'Where are you going?' he asked. I told him I was going to Naranjo and he wanted to know why. It must have seemed strange to him that this young white woman was out there in the forest alone, and even stranger that she was heading for a Tsachila community. I explained that I was going to Augustine's house to teach a class. 'Are you a *hermana*?' he asked. I thought he was using the Spanish word for 'sister' in the sense in which evangelicals in Ecuador use it, addressing each other as 'brother' or 'sister'. Looking back now, I think he was really asking whether I was a Catholic nun! I said yes, anyway, and he wished me well and Godspeed. I breathed a slight sigh of relief and continued on my way.

It was late afternoon when I returned by the same route on my way back to Cóngoma. I was tired, hot and sticky and the bugs had feasted on my bare arms, and I just wanted to get back to my little wooden house, grab some clean clothes and go down to the river for a cool swim. As Roobarb plodded up a steep incline, a voice called out from a bamboo house standing on stilts in a clearing beside the trail: '*Hermana!* Won't you stop a while and have something to drink with us?' I looked across and saw a young woman waving and calling to me from an open window. A smiling man appeared at her side and I recognized him as the *Manaba* from that morning. A young boy ran down the steps at the side of the house and indicated that I should dismount and go up to join them. The prospect of a cool drink and some shade for a while was appealing and I barely considered the wisdom of going into a stranger's house in the middle of the forest.

I handed my reins to the boy, who couldn't have been more than seven, and climbed the rough wooden stairs to the house. Inside, I could see that a huge effort had been made to create a home in those humble surroundings, with colourful cloths on the table and cushions on the chairs. The man told me that his name was Enrique Cassanova and he introduced me to his wife and family. I felt very welcome and they proceeded to treat me as an honoured guest. Within a few minutes, a steaming bowl of soup was placed on the table in front of me, followed by a plate of delicious chicken and rice. I realized that this family was showing me the greatest hospitality, to the point of sacrificing one of their valuable birds to feed me. I washed the feast down with lemonade. I couldn't think why they were being so generous.

Once I had eaten my fill, the table was cleared and the family gathered round. To my astonishment, Enrique asked me to tell them how they could know God. He said they were Catholic but they didn't know how they could learn about God and they really wanted to. He asked me whether I would be willing to teach them. Sometimes I am amazed at the way the Holy Spirit works in people's hearts. This man living in a humble home in the Ecuadorian rainforest had been touched by God's Spirit and had conceived a desire to have a relationship with him. As Isaiah 65:1 says:

> I revealed myself to those who did not ask for me;
> I was found by those who did not seek me.
>   To a nation that did not call on my name,
>   I said, 'Here am I, here am I.'

From that day on, I routinely stopped at Enrique's home on my way back from teaching in Naranjo. We enjoyed many meals together and I led Bible studies with the family for many months. Eventually, they moved into town and I later learnt that they did come to faith in Christ and were baptized and welcomed into the Baptist church there. Such is the grace and mercy of God in human lives!

The issue of wanting to be useful was one I continued to struggle with in Cóngoma, just as I had in Naranjo. 'What am I doing here?' I often asked myself. I would tell myself that God knew what I was doing there; but sometimes even that certainty was not enough to stop me being tormented by my apparent uselessness. Like many people, my sense of my own worth is tied up with what I *do* and although I realize that God is primarily interested in the kind of person I am, deep down I know that my worth is dependent on who *he* is and what *he* thinks of me – a member of 'a royal priesthood, a holy nation, God's special possession'. His child.

In an effort to be more useful and do more 'missionary-like' things, I began to spend more time in Santo Domingo. I got involved in the Spanish-speaking church there – *El Buen Pastor*, the Good Shepherd Church – working with the youth group. I took my turn teaching at the weekly women's meeting. I also continued visiting the Tsachila communities, now by motorcycle. I rode a trail bike which was ideal for muddy tracks and shallow river crossings – my days as a biker served me well and I loved handling the machine in those difficult terrains. I could get around all seven Tsachila communities easily and quickly now and my circle of contacts among these people grew.

Before long, I moved back into town. It had been hard for me living out in the rainforest with no 'ex-pat' company, so I enjoyed sharing a little wooden house with Jane, who at that time was working among a small group of highland Quechua people who lived in Santo Domingo. It was great having a roommate – especially one who was as much fun as she was! We spent a lot of time doubled up laughing at the tales we both had to tell.

One day, Jane came back from a trip to the mountains. She had been in Riobamba, which is the capital of Chimborazo Province. A huge demonstration had been taking place that day, she told me, and as she was standing on the kerb watching hundreds of people – including soldiers and policemen – marching past, it had dawned on her that it was an anti-US protest. People were waving their fists in the air and shouting: '*Los Americanos abajo! Abajo!* – Down with the Americans! Down, down!' She became very conscious of her white skin, blue eyes and blond hair and for a moment she wondered whether she was in any danger. Then she noticed that the men marching by were staring at her, hissing to get her attention and calling softly: 'Hey, *gringita guapa!* – Hey, beautiful little gringa!' She laughed as she realized that their propensity for flirting was way stronger than their political convictions!

Another funny incident involved Doreen. Arriving back very tired from a trip to Quevedo, we had been planning to flop down and rest as soon as we got home. As we reached our patio, Doreen appeared from her house next door, her hair dishevelled and her voice a few notes higher than normal. '*Me muero!*' she began. 'Well! We've been *invaded!* It's dreadful! Dreadful!' She was clearly very agitated. Before either of us could say a word, she declared: 'We must pray!'

Closing her eyes, she bowed her head and embarked on a long and fervent prayer about *los invasores*, 'the invaders'. Jane and I stood looking at each other in bewilderment, unable to join her in prayer, unable even to make sense of what she was saying. Our bewilderment turned to stifled mirth as we signed to each other: Where were these aliens that had invaded our planet? We were almost crying with laughter by the time she concluded with a loud 'Amen!' and opened her eyes. She was obviously unhappy that we were not taking this crisis seriously.

It took only a few minutes then to get to the bottom of the mystery. In Ecuador, it is common for groups of squatters to take over disused pieces of land and claim them by putting up wooden shacks and moving in. There are whole suburbs that have developed out of what were originally squatter settlements. The people who do this are known as *invasores* and their encampments are called *invasiones*. Neither Jane nor I had been familiar with these terms and so when Doreen in distress tried to tell us that a small group of squatters had moved onto some adjoining land, all we could think of was little green men with antennae sticking out of their heads!

It turned out not to be a big issue, however. The squatters were quickly moved on and peace was restored once they had gone.

While I was living in Santo Domingo, I had the opportunity to join a group of women from the church who visited the local prison. Prisons in Ecuador are not like those in Britain, and nor is the justice system like Britain's – people can be held without trial for many months. Santo Domingo's prison was horrendously overcrowded at the time, with forty or fifty men cooped up in each small cell for twenty-four hours a day. There was no exercise yard. Nor were there any showers or toilets, and the stench of unwashed bodies mingling with the slop buckets was overpowering. Men slept on pieces of cardboard on the floor. Nothing was provided for them – they had to rely on their relatives to bring them not just toiletries and clean clothes but even food and water. Prisoners from out of town depended on the generosity of other inmates – or took what they needed from those weaker than themselves.

Once a week, this little group of women took in food and water and, more importantly (as we thought), also took the word of God to share. We would stand in the corridor outside the cells and sing, and the prisoners (who got to know the songs well and even requested their favourites) would join in. Then, someone would preach a message of forgiveness and hope through Jesus Christ and follow that by offering to pray with anyone who wanted to turn away from his sinful way of life.

Every week, men would drop to their knees right there in the filth and ask God for forgiveness and salvation. It seemed that so many had hit rock bottom in that place – a living hell – and were desperate to change. We prayed with them and gave out leaflets and Bibles with simple courses of study they could do, which we hoped would help them understand the significance of that moment in their lives. Many tears were shed, by them and by us as we saw the miracle of God's redemption right before our eyes. Over the years that followed, we had the joy of maintaining contact with some of those men who went on to live very different lives, and we witnessed their transformation and reintegration into society.

After the preaching and praying were over – and only then – we served them food. Usually, it was simple fare, such as bread and cheese and Coca-Cola, though sometimes one of the local restaurants gave us huge pots of *arróz con pollo* (chicken with rice) to distribute. The prisoners were grateful whatever they got, and very appreciative.

One week, it was my turn to preach. Normally, the men settled quickly after the singing and even those who were not interested kept a respectful silence so the others could hear; but on this occasion one man was very disruptive, talking loudly in the background and even calling out. I found it very distracting. The other men in his cell tried to quieten him down but he became louder and louder and finally came to the door of the cell and started shouting at me. He seemed very aggressive. As other inmates tried to pull him away from the bars, a scuffle broke out.

The noise made it impossible to continue and I stopped speaking. I was surprised and disturbed, unsure what to do next. I said a silent prayer: 'What am I doing here? God, please bring peace and order!' The angry man pushed his way to the bars again and looked straight at me. His words shocked me. 'How can I listen to you? I can't hear you, I'm too hungry. My stomach is in pain. I don't need preaching, I need food!'

The raw truth of those words hit me and in that moment my life was changed. 'I can't hear you, I'm too hungry. I don't need preaching, I need food.' It brought home to me in a new way that the gospel is more than words. God's love can and should be communicated not only in Bible readings, sermons and testimonies but in actions. 'For God so loved the world that he *gave . . .*' Love in action. From that day onwards, we fed the prisoners *before* we preached to them.

That incident had a profound effect on me. I started to look long and hard at the Gospels to see how Jesus approached people. Over and over again, I saw that he was very practical: when they were hungry, he fed them; when they were sick, he healed them – body, soul and spirit. Yes, he preached and yes, he taught – but first he met the needs that people felt most keenly.

I'd already noticed that when the mobile medical team from the HCJB (in 2014 HCJB changed its name to Reach Beyond – so all further references will be to Reach Beyond) hospital in Quito visited the Tsachila, folk would flock to their clinics. Good medical and dental treatment was not easily accessible out in the rainforest, and in town it was expensive to see a doctor and buy medicine. The Reach Beyond team had good doctors who treated people with respect and kindness. Each evening, they showed films about basic health and hygiene and gave talks on how to stay healthy. They also sang, did health quizzes for the children and shared their testimonies before concluding with a film on the life of Christ. In other words, they attended to both physical and spiritual needs. I loved it when they came and often volunteered to translate for them. I also learnt to take people's blood pressure, temperature and pulse. It felt good to be part of the team – and to be *doing something useful.*

When the medical team visited, I noticed that certain members of the community who were usually antagonistic to the gospel showed up each evening for the meetings. They sat through the songs and the testimonies and watched the films with rapt attention. Granted, at that time there was no electricity in Cóngoma and so this was all hugely entertaining for them – but the point was that they joined in everything. Their physical needs were being met and it seemed that this opened a door for spiritual input, too. Wow! This was a powerful lesson for me.

I knew then that I needed to add other skills to my knowledge of the Bible. After much prayer and deliberation, I resolved that I would train to become a nurse. And so it was that in July 1989 I wept my way across the Atlantic, heartbroken at leaving my beloved Ecuador but knowing I would be going back, to the place God had called me. First, though, East Birmingham School of Nursing awaited me, and four years of hard work and study.

8

I Used to Spear Others – Now You Spear Me!

As I came off duty for the last time in November 1993, I was filled with mixed emotions. My three years of study at East Birmingham Hospital had passed quickly and I had enjoyed immensely my first job as a staff nurse on a busy medical ward, and yet I felt elated as I headed to the store to turn in my five uniforms, my nurse's cape and my keys. I had finished the course and was now ready to begin work as a missionary nurse with Reach Beyond (RB).

However, my high spirits were tempered by the sadness I felt at leaving my mother again. Over the last four years we had become very close. All my friends knew Mum and loved her, and she was often included in our trips and holidays. For her part, she loved having us around and cooked wonderful meals for us all. More important, she, too, had come to faith in Christ and so we were able to encourage each other and pray for each other. I was going to miss her love and friendship every bit as much as she would miss me.

I landed in Quito a week later. My plan was to live at first with Brenda Greenslade, a fellow Brit who rented a large flat close to the mission hospital. As I didn't need any household appliances or kitchen supplies of my own, I was carrying all my possessions in two suitcases. I felt very excited but also a little apprehensive. Did I have enough clinical experience? Would I be able to handle medical Spanish? How would I get on with my teammates?

My work assignment was not yet decided. I had corresponded with the head of RB's department for community health and development, but no definite decision had been made as to where I would best fit. I knew that I wanted to be in close contact with the Tsachila but I also knew that the mission would deploy me in one of its own projects, or 'ministries'.

It felt good to be back in Quito. It is a beautiful city, surrounded by four volcanoes: Cayambe, Cotopaxi and Antisana, all snow-capped, and the green slopes of Pichincha. Its people, like all Ecuadorians, are by nature friendly and warm to strangers, and I love their customs and their delicious food!

I discovered that I also enjoyed being part of a larger, mul-tinational mission community. The RB compound was like a small, self-contained village, except that nobody actually lived on site. There was always plenty of activity, people coming and going, and endless visitors. There was a mechanic's shop where mission vehicles were repaired, and a printing department that produced Bibles and other literature. Graphic artists designed letterheads, leaflets, newsletters, cards and even magazines to support the mission's work, while a small army of support staff worked in accounting, administration, information technology, hospitality and personnel.

Many of my new colleagues were involved in broadcasting the good news of Jesus to the world on shortwave radio, and every day programmes were being made in French, German, Russian, Portuguese, Swedish, Czech and Japanese as well as English, Spanish and Kichwa. These were beamed to the very top of Pichincha and then bounced from there to an 'antenna farm' about 20 miles from Quito, from which they were directed all around the world. It was a grand operation that required teams of engineers working round the clock to maintain all the necessary equipment.

At our weekly staff meetings, we often heard wonderful stories of lives changed as people responded to the messages they heard on the radio. Every day, a truck brought sacks of letters. 'We are more than a radio station, we are friends who care' was the tag line used on the English broadcasts and many listeners did indeed feel that the staff at the station were friends who cared about them and they would send in prayer requests and photographs of their families and pets.

My own world, however, was across the street from the studios. Hospital Vozandes (it shared the name of the radio station, which means 'Voice of the Andes') had opened in the 1950s to care for the needs both of missionary staff and of the Kichwa people who lived in the countryside round about. Its doctors and nurses came from the United States, Canada, New Zealand and Britain, and provided compassionate care and treatment to people who came from all over Ecuador seeking help. In those days, there had been few health facilities in Quito. Originally, the hospital was quite basic and had just fifty beds, but in the eighties it was expanded to seventy beds plus four operating theatres and a seven-bed intensive care unit. The hospital is now a major trauma centre for the city of Quito and one of the finest training hospitals in the country.

Reach Beyond established a second, smaller hospital after Vozandes was completed, a wooden structure in a place named Shell (after the oil company, which had built a long airstrip there to facilitate its efforts to drill in the nearby Amazon rainforest). The staff at that hospital had served the people of the forest for more than half a century until it was closed in

2013. The provision of free medical care at a new government hospital just 8 kilometres away indicated to us that this aspect of our ministry in Shell was completed.

In addition to the hospitals, RB staff were involved in community health and development in rural parts of the country. Every other week, sturdy vehicles transported doctors and dentists high into the Andes, out to the subtropical coastlands and even into the fringes of the rainforest, where they would be taken by canoe to attend to the needs of the tribal people there. In those days, the mandate was to reach out to people where they lived, right in their own communities.

Along with providing medical care, staff would explain to the country folk how they could look after their own health. Inevitably, the question of clean water arose, because a lot of the patients at our mobile unit displayed symptoms of intestinal parasite infection with diarrhoeal diseases, which in small children was especially serious. Discussion would usually turn to ways to improve and protect local water sources and, in those communities that were motivated to take action, RB workers would get involved.

The water and sanitation staff in the mission's community health and development department were always busy. They worked with communities all over Ecuador to provide drinkable water in some of the most remote areas of the country. In the mountains, they looked for springs that could meet the needs of nearby villages and then, with the help of local people, their technicians would secure them from contamination by humans or animals. They carried out topographical surveys to measure the elevation of each spring and of the houses it was to supply and would then draw a plan to show how the water could be carried downhill to the village through PVC pipes, which were buried for protection.

Digging the trenches required was hard labour. They had to be almost one-and-a-half metres deep and half a metre wide, and they could be as much as five kilometres in length! Everyone who was going to benefit from the new water supply was expected to do their share of digging – men and women, old people, even children. They worked hard in spite of the thin air. At altitudes of 3,500 metres or more, our ex-pat teams could barely lift their shovels and it was soon obvious that a single elderly Kichwa woman would achieve fifty times as much as a foreigner in a day! However, the local people were gracious and welcomed our valiant efforts to help, and generously shared their food with us: potatoes, broad beans, corn and (as a special treat) guinea pig. In this way, we were able to build strong relationships with these people which provided openings to share God's love with them.

For the first couple of years after my return to Ecuador, I was privileged to work on all of the mission's community health and development projects. I served with the mobile unit, taught health and hygiene with the water project team, was airlifted into the rainforest to train health promoters alongside older and more experienced nurses, and even got to work with a research team investigating the transmission and treatment of onchocerciasis, or 'river blindness', and other tropical diseases.

It was an exciting and fulfilling time. I finally felt I was 'being useful'. I felt like a real missionary. I was 'helping people' and at the same time I had opportunities to talk to them about Jesus. I *knew* what I was doing there and I loved my life.

One day, my boss at the time, Dr Carlos Feijoo, called me into his office and told me that we were sending vaccination teams to some remote areas of the rainforest. One such area was a Waorani protectorate that was closed to everyone who didn't have both explicit permission from the government and clearance from the oil company that was working there. The company had carved a road through the forest to transport its heavy equipment, so it was now possible to drive there – and we could stay in the camps the *petroleros* had built there.

He asked me whether I would be willing to go. Would I? Yes, please! Yes! Yes! Please could I go? I was even more excited when he told me I would be accompanying Pat Kelley, a legendary trainer of native teachers who had worked with the Waorani for many years and spoke their language, Waotidido, fluently and understood their customs. In spite of our difference in age – she is at least ten years older than me – Pat is a good friend and the prospect of travelling with her and learning from her was way more than I could have dreamt of.

I learnt that we would have to make several trips to the same area to complete the programme. The oil company, which had access to helicopters for transportation and refrigerators for storage, would be handling the difficult task of keeping the vaccines cool enough, in the heat and humidity of the forest, to remain effective. My role was simply to drive the car and administer the vaccines, nothing more. Pat would take responsibility for everything else: public relations, record-keeping, translation – and ensuring our survival!

A few weeks later, we set out from Quito on our great adventure. We never imagined how great an adventure it would prove to be.

The road from Quito to the eastern rainforest of Ecuador (otherwise known as 'the Oriente') climbs over the wild *páramo*, a high, treeless plateau, to the continental divide near a place called Papallácta. At its highest point, it reaches over 3,800 metres above sea level. In the 1990s, parts of this road still consisted of gravel with no tarmac and were in a pretty poor state. There was no way to go fast and so, when not avoiding potholes large enough to swallow a small herd of llamas, I admired the scenery surrounding us. Rocky crags towered above us, waves of colour flowed over the windswept grass, waterfalls splashed down onto the road and always we were expecting to see condors flying overhead or to catch a glimpse of one of the snow-capped peaks in the distance.

Conversation with Pat was always easy and relaxed but we were also comfortable with long periods of silence and personal reflection. We simply enjoyed each other's company – for me, she was a perfect travelling companion. She was happy to pull up at any 'hole in the wall' for a meal, so we never had to search for a suitable place to eat, we just stopped when we were hungry. The first day on the road was uneventful and we stopped for the night in the town of Lago Agrio.

The next morning, we set out early as we still had a long journey ahead of us. Pat was anxious to get to the protectorate before nightfall, in time to find a place to stay. She did not want to be associated with the oil company and so there was no question of accepting its hospitality in any of its camps. Instead, we would stay with a Waorani family. First, however, we had to cross a nearby river, the Rio Aguarico, on a commercial ferry.

As we pulled up near the water's edge, I could see that the ferry was already full. It was a rusty old tub which could take at most fifteen vehicles. As I was calculating how it would affect our plans if we missed this crossing, a man stepped forward and shouted at me to drive on. He pointed to a space at the back where the pick-up would just fit. Without another thought, I did as he said. There wasn't a proper ramp but I managed to get down the steep bank from the road onto the shore and then up onto the ferry without catching our undercarriage on anything. We breathed a sigh of shared relief as I cut the engine and put on the handbrake. We were still on schedule.

The crossing was quick – about thirty minutes. The ferry was already turning to back into the opposite bank when the man collecting the fares approached me. As I was getting out some money, the lorry in front of us started up and jumped back a metre or so, crashing into the front of the pick-up. 'What the heck?' I thought. Momentarily dazed, it took a few seconds for me to realize what had happened. The driver had not been aware of the small pick-up behind him and had begun to reverse onto the shore. Only the jolt and the noise of crumpling steel, along with the shouts of the other drivers, had stopped him from shunting us right off the boat.

I got out to inspect the damage. The bonnet was buckled and bent up, the bumper had partly come off and the headlights were smashed. It could have been a lot worse. The lorry driver came over and ran his eye over it. '*No es nada*,' he mumbled. 'It's nothing.' By that time, the rush of adrenalin that kicks in after a shock had taken effect and I was incensed. '*No es nada?*' I yelled. '*No es nada?! Mira lo que ha hecho!* It's nothing? It's nothing?! Look what you've done!' Ignoring my angry remonstrations, the man climbed up into his cab and shouted: '*Muévase!* Move!'

Sometimes when I look back and reflect on some of the more stupid things I have done in my life, this occasion comes to mind. I was so indignant that I decided I was *not* going to move – thereby blocking the exit for all the other vehicles. It was a stand-off.

Pat looked at me. 'You're not going to move?' she asked incredulously. 'No,' I said. 'Not till he pays for the damage.' By this time, a crowd had gathered. Some were the drivers of the other vehicles on the ferry, some were drivers of vehicles waiting to board it for the journey back, many others were merely onlookers amused by the impasse and wondering what would happen next. And then there was the host of vendors selling fried plantain, Coke, corn and chewing gum.

Stubbornness is not a good attribute. At first, the crowd took my side and added their voices to my insistence that the lorry driver was at fault and of course must pay for the damage to the pick-up. I smiled as I waited in the afternoon heat for him to comply. 'I'm not paying!' was his response. Soon, the other drivers began to lose patience. They wanted to get on with their journeys. They had goods to deliver or collect, meetings to attend. '*Señorita*,' they said, 'just drive off the ferry. Of course he has to pay. It was clearly his fault. We will back you up.' But there was no way I was going to give up my advantage.

People then became angry with me. 'Move the pick-up!' they shouted. 'We're wasting time. We need to get on. You're holding everyone up.' The ferry captain came over and told me it was an offence to block the exit and I would be heavily fined if I didn't move my vehicle. That was enough to persuade me to reverse onto the shore – and then stop, still blocking the way for everyone else. 'I'm off the ferry now,' I announced.

The lorry driver was now coming under heavy verbal fire from the fickle crowd as they swung back from trying to get me to move to trying to get him to pay. Pat stood to one side among the crowd of onlookers, a slight smile playing occasionally on her worried face as she watched.

Finally, the lorry driver came over to me and confessed that he had no money but his cargo was crates of beer. How much did I think it would cost to repair the damage? I suggested a figure, largely plucked out of the air. We haggled and finally came to an agreement. He placed some crates of beer in the back of the pick-up, to the value we had settled on, and I followed him to the nearest town, where he sold them and paid me in full.

We parted then with an amicable handshake and Pat and I laughed all the way to the Waorani community, hardly believing that I could have been so stubborn and maybe so stupid! We had also sneaked a photo of a mission vehicle loaded with beer. That would be a story to tell!

Arriving at our destination late that afternoon, we were greeted by Wepe, a member of the community who was at least seventy years old. His ear lobes, lengthened in the traditional way, hung almost to his shoulders, his long, black hair was loose and he was dressed in nothing but an old pair of shorts and some Wellington boots. The toothless grin he greeted us with stretched from ear to ear. 'Kawo!' he exclaimed, greeting Pat by her tribal name. '*Wapone!* It's good to see you!'

Wepe was one of the old-style Waorani who had seen so much change in their lifetimes. He had once been a nomadic hunter, roaming the rainforest, living in fear of other Waorani who sought to kill him and himself seeking revenge on others who had killed members of his family. The Waorani have been described as the most murderous tribe on the planet and much has been written about their endless cycles of bloodshed.

After the brutal spearing of five young US missionaries in 1956, Elisabeth Elliot and Rachel Saint (whose husband and brother respectively had been among the dead) went to live with the tribe – a story well documented in Elliot's book, *Through Gates of Splendour.*[2] Most of the Waorani then decided to settle and live in peace and community, but Wepe had been one of the so-called 'down-river' group that had opted to retain their nomadic ways and keep away from outsiders. Years later, however, he had resolved after all to follow the path of peace and 'walk God's trail'. Now he lived in the protectorate, where there were still plenty of monkeys and wild boars to hunt and fish to catch.

When he saw the damage to the pick-up, Wepe's smile disappeared. 'What happened?' he demanded furiously. Pat proceeded to tell the whole story in Waotidido. The Waorani love a good tale and before long an audience had gathered. As they listened, they expressed their indignation at the lorry driver's attitude, their approval of my refusal to give way and their amusement at what transpired. It got very noisy as everyone spoke at once. I didn't altogether understand what was going on and the clamour was making me a bit nervous, when suddenly Wepe leapt up and shouted something, his face dark with anger.

Everyone went quiet. What was happening? Although many Waorani now 'walk God's trail', some still have a reputation for being volatile and unpredictable. So do many of us, of course – but in their case rage can lead to extreme violence and even murder. Pat said a few stern words and Wepe sat down with a rueful grin, muttering something. Everyone relaxed. She went on with her story.

Afterwards, I asked her to tell me what had provoked such anger in Wepe and what had defused it so quickly. She said he was incensed that the lorry driver had refused to pay up and had vowed that he was going to get his spear and hunt him down and kill him! She had reminded him that walking God's trail meant that we did not take revenge like that anymore. Wepe had calmed down, but what he had muttered was 'Well, I'm going to ask God if it's OK and if it is, I'm going to spear him!'

The very next day, I had the task of 'spearing' Wepe. There is no word for 'vaccinate' in Waotidido, so the Waorani in their logical way use the verb 'to spear'. It was no wonder that part of the challenge for me and Pat was to catch our patients in the first place! Small children would hear that the *cowode*, the outsiders, were coming to spear them and would take off into the forest. Older children, who understood what vaccination was, had to run them down like bounty hunters and drag them back kicking and screaming. Nothing I could do or say would dispel their fear, so I just had to be quick with my needle.

Wepe, however, had the last word. As he sat before me waiting for his injection, he flexed his still muscular arm and grinned. 'I used to spear others, now you are spearing me!' We laughed together.

9

You Like Surgery, Right?

In those early years, I was also asked to help with a variety of other projects. One of these was a programme to combat blindness in the far north of Ecuador, almost at the border with Colombia.

In the early nineties, there was no access by road to the town of San Lorenzo, which could be reached only by train, by river or by air. The train, or *ferrocarril*, was essentially a bus on rails which made the daily trip from Ibarra, north of Quito, and took anything from ten to twenty hours to reach San Lorenzo owing to frequent breakdowns and derailments. You sat on top of the carriage to take advantage of the natural air-conditioning, which made the tortuous journey down from the mountains a beautiful if uncomfortable adventure. You did it once, for fun, but never again if you could possibly avoid it.

Canoes and motorboats arrived frequently from the town of Borbón, which was roughly an eight-to-twelve-hour drive from Quito depending on the state of the road. The third option was to fly in to a landing strip situated about 10 kilometres from San Lorenzo. There were no commercial flights, so Mission Aviation Fellowship laid on a plane as and when requested.

Reach Beyond had opened a small eye clinic in San Lorenzo. The province of Esmeraldas in which the town is situated is one of the poorest and most neglected in Ecuador. The south is flourishing, as its beautiful beaches bring in foreign tourists and Quiteños at holiday time, but the north is too close to Colombia and the guerrilla war there, and is anyway inaccessible by road. What is more, its coastline is fringed with mangrove swamps and although to the ecologist these are a paradise rich in biodiversity, to tourists they mean only one thing: malaria!

'So, will you go?' asked Dr Feijoo. He wanted me to accompany an Ecuadorian ophthalmologist to San Lorenzo for four days. 'You won't have to do anything, just observe and then write a report for me,' he explained. I had been about to protest that I knew absolutely nothing about eyes and couldn't see how I could possibly be helpful; but now I had no excuse. Yes, I could go and, yes, I could observe and, yes, I could write a report.

The following Thursday, I showed up at the small hangar at the far end of Quito's International airport where Mission Aviation Fellowship (MAF) kept its red-and-white Cessna plane. We weighed in – our luggage, ourselves and the supplies we were taking to the clinic – and clambered aboard and strapped ourselves in. The ophthalmologist, a Dr Carlos Yepez, had a pleasant demeanour and seemed like a nice man, though I was a little anxious in case he should think I was going to be of any use at all and then be disappointed!

The little plane raced down the runway and took to the clear blue sky, vibrating alarmingly as it climbed steeply to clear the mountains to the north of the city. After that, it would be 'downhill all the way' as we descended to sea level. 'So,' said Dr Yepez, attempting to make conversation, 'you're interested in eyes?' I confessed that I wasn't especially. 'But you like surgery, right?' He seemed to be looking for reassurance. 'Er, no, not really,' I replied. He looked at me closely. 'Ah, but you will!' he said decisively.

We touched down, almost exactly an hour later, with a succession of bumps. It felt to me like we were landing in a ploughed field, though it actually was a proper airstrip. There was not a soul in sight. All around was dense green forest – only the tall trees had been cut around the strip, for safety, but everything else looked like 'virgin jungle'.

Once the propeller had come to a stop, we undid our harnesses and climbed out onto the grass. A couple of minutes later, we were standing at the edge of the airstrip alongside our small pile of cargo. The heat and humidity were overpowering and I was already bathed in sweat. Yuk! How was I going to endure four days of this, I wondered.

In the distance we could hear the sound of an approaching vehicle. I was to learn later that while there was no road *to* San Lorenzo, there was a road network *within* the town and a stretch of 15 kilometres outside it had been levelled and gravelled in anticipation of the day when the road from Quito would eventually be built. Every car and lorry in the town had literally been shipped in on the river.

Some minutes later, a battered brown four-by-four emerged from the forest and pulled up beside us and a strikingly handsome young black man jumped out. Jorge Arroyo was an employee of the clinic. He greeted us warmly with handshakes and hugs and then handed a cool box to the pilot. 'Your shrimps,' he said. That part of the coast is famous for its jumbo shrimps and the pilot's family in Quito would be feasting on some that very night. Maybe that was why he waggled his wings as the Cessna took off!

The final leg of the journey to San Lorenzo was brutal. The way was little more than a track and every few metres we would hit a bone-jarring hole. It was a huge relief when we finally drew up beside a concrete building with what seemed like two hundred people waiting outside it. We had arrived at the clinic.

I don't think I had even wondered what an eye clinic might look like before the moment I found out. If I had, I don't think I would have pictured anything like what I saw. The crowd around the door parted to let us through and we entered a large waiting-room. Wooden benches ran around the walls and there was a desk at one end. Behind it was a second room that passed for an operating theatre. There was no air-conditioning and it was hardly sterile, but it was kept as clean as possible and the patients were given gowns, and socks to cover their feet.

A smiling-faced young woman greeted us and Jorge introduced me to Maruja Ante, the clinic's other employee. Up to that point, I had prided myself on my fluency in Spanish. I had a good accent and seldom had a problem either understanding native speakers or making myself understood. That was until I went to San Lorenzo. Ecuadorian coastal Spanish is different to the highland Spanish in that on the coast they don't pronounce the letter 's'. In San Lorenzo, they don't seem to articulate any other letters either! I had the hardest job to comprehend anything Jorge or Maruja said.

San Lorenzeños (as they're called) also use a whole variety of words you won't hear anywhere else in Ecuador. For example, in the clinic we used a slit lamp for eye examinations. The patient rests their chin on a plate and looks straight ahead. The Spanish word for 'chin' that I had learnt was *quijada*, but in San Lorenzo it is *mentón* or *cumbamba*. Jorge and Maruja dissolved into laughter at my surprise when they told me to put my *cumbamba* on the plate. I wasn't sure which part of my anatomy they were referring to!

That first day was an eye-opener in every sense. I was astonished to discover that Jorge and Maruja had no formal training in either medicine or nursing. The clinic had been set up by a German ophthalmic nurse and she had taught them both to treat simple eye infections and minor traumas, measure people for glasses and screen them for glaucoma. They also selected the patients for cataract surgery and then gave them post-operative care. Juana Beck had obviously been a good teacher and had chosen her staff well. Jorge and Maruja were diligent and had become extremely knowledgeable about their field. As committed Christians, they showed love for their people and had a passion to share Christ with them. As natives of San Lorenzo, they knew everyone in town.

I learnt a lot as I watched while each patient was examined by Dr Yepez. Before our arrival, Jorge and Maruja had screened them all and tested their eyesight. They had also prepared each one with eye-drops to dilate their pupils so that the doctor could look inside their eyes without delay.

Some of the patients needed to be seen by Dr Yepez because they had conditions that Jorge and Maruja couldn't deal with. Others had come for post-operative check-ups. Some had cataracts that were scheduled for surgery the next day. More than sixty people were seen that first day and we were still working as night fell.

Eventually, Jorge drove us to our hotel. I was so exhausted by the heat, the clamour of the waiting patients and the sheer length of the day that I simply wanted to fall into bed. After a cold shower, I did just that, ready for a very early start the next morning.

I have to acknowledge that Dr Yepez had been right. I did become fascinated by eyes and I came to love surgery. On my first day in the makeshift theatre, I had watched my first cataract operation. Dr Yepez had patiently explained every step of the procedure, from the nerve-block anaesthesia to the incision, the removal of the clouded lens, the insertion of a synthetic lens and finally the sewing-up, using suture as fine as a human hair. The teaching microscope he was using had two sets of eyepieces and he had let me watch up-close as he performed surgery so delicate and skilful that I was left in awe. To my amazement, after each operation the patient got up and walked out unaided. They went home to rest with drops for their eyes and instructions to come back on the Sunday for a check-up.

After I had watched two such operations, I was scrubbed up and ready to assist with the third. So began my 'career' as an ophthalmic theatre nurse. Over the next four years, I was to make the trip to San Lorenzo every month and assist Dr Yepez in many hundreds of operations. I never lost the sense of wonder, the sense of fulfilment, the pure emotion that made me weep as we removed the eye patches from patients who had previously been blinded by cataracts and they exclaimed, crying themselves: '*Puedo ver!* I can see!'

Eventually, I moved into a leadership position in the community development department. I continued to help at the clinic each month but now I was determined that our patients and staff deserved a better facility. There was land available and so we drew up plans for a purpose-built clinic. I had no idea how its construction could be funded, but I laid it all before God in prayer, knowing that he is Jehovah Jireh, the great provider who could furnish us with all the finance we needed.

The new San Lorenzo clinic was dedicated in the summer of 1999. A grant from Jersey Overseas Aid had paid for everything. Over the years since then, many thousands of people have had their sight restored by surgery there. The road to San Lorenzo was completed shortly after. The *ferrocarril* no longer runs and the journey to San Lorenzo from Quito now takes only half a day. That's what I call 'progress'.

10

A Normal Life? Not for Me!

Three long staccato bursts of gunfire, from somewhere high above us in the mountains, jerked me from my daydream. In an instant, I was back in the moment. I was caught in a hold-up. I had been robbed. I was in fear for my life. My heart began to race again.

The sun was high in the sky. Two hours and more had passed since I had arrived at that spot and I was thirsty, hungry, hot – and very scared. 'What am I doing here, Lord?' I prayed. Then, complaining: 'Why couldn't I have a more normal life? A regular job, a salary, holidays like everyone else? Why do I have to do *this*?' Just as I was starting to wallow in self-pity, I heard a shout: '*Ya se fueron!* They've gone!'

Evidently, the gunfire was the signal that the hold-up was over. The tractor-trailer that was blocking the road roared into life and the driver started to manoeuvre it out of our way. On all sides, people were getting out of their vehicles and yelling and crying and gesticulating and hugging each other in relief. I climbed out of the pick-up and at once was surrounded by well-meaning folk anxious to make sure that I was unharmed. I was the only foreigner around – and a woman at that and on my own. The consensus was that, judging by their accents, our assailants were members of the *Fuerzas Armadas Revolucionarias de Colombia*, the guerrilla movement known as 'Farc'. Everyone agreed that we were lucky we had not been killed. We were all grateful that everyone had given up their money and their valuables without attempting any resistance.

My only thought now was to get away from that place. As soon as the road ahead was open again, I set off, very glad (given that all my money had been taken) that I had filled my tank with petrol before leaving San Lorenzo. I 'drove like Jehu' up into the mountains, swinging around the bends with tyres squealing. I had the CD player on and when a Sandi Patty song about God's power to protect us came on, the emotional floodgates opened and I wept uncontrollably, sobbing and gasping for air as the sense of relief overwhelmed me. I shouted at God, too, to let out all my pent-up feelings.

At the first checkpoint on the road into the town of Ibarra, the police asked me for my papers. They were oblivious to my distress, my eyes red from crying – they just wanted to see my licence! I heard a voice screaming at them, and realized it was mine. 'I have no papers, no licence, and no passport – and where were *you* when we were all being held up at gunpoint just down the road?' It was an outburst born as much out of the exhilaration of my relief as out of all the fear I had felt earlier. 'I wondered why no cars were coming through,' said the younger of the two policemen, and received another tirade from me. His companion wisely said: 'Just let her go!'

In Ibarra, I finally got a cellphone signal and was able to call the office. A couple of hours later, I reached the shelter of the house I shared with Jane. She was waiting for me with her lovely parents. A wonderful meal was on the table and the room was full of flowers. My anxious colleagues at the mission had sent roses – it was St Valentine's Day or, as we say in Ecuador, 'the Day of Love and Friendship' and I certainly felt the strength of their love and friendship then. I finally felt safe. I was home.

Part 2

11

We *Can* Do Something

The 26 December 2004 may not be a date inscribed in many people's minds, but some of us at least will never forget 'the day of the tsunami'. The very word 'tsunami' was hardly understood back then, and it certainly wasn't often used; but who doesn't remember seeing images of the enormous waves that engulfed beachside hotels, houses and cars, and even entire towns, and killed over 220,000 people that day?

It was Boxing Day in Britain. I was on home leave, visiting my younger sister, June, and her family. After a brisk walk in the Lincolnshire countryside, we had gathered to enjoy the leftovers from Christmas when someone switched on the television. I vividly recall watching the horrifying footage on the news. Much of it had been shot by amateurs – after all, why would the BBC or anyone else be covering just another day on the beach in south-east Asia?

As reports of the vast extent of the devastation and loss of life came in over the days that followed, I began to wonder whether there was anything practical I could do. Reach Beyond had been active for years in the Asia-Pacific region, helping local people to set up small community radio stations, but we had no medical work there, no medical team on the ground nearby or any relief workers we could deploy to the affected areas. To date, all our medical work had been based in Ecuador, in Quito and Shell.

The story continued to unfold day by day, with harrowing accounts of immense destruction and people missing, presumed dead, in Indonesia, Thailand and Sri Lanka. I had started to look for ways I could volunteer to help when my boss, Curt Cole, called from the USA: 'Is there anything Reach Beyond can do?'

'Yes,' I said. 'We can definitely put a medical team together to do something. We'll need to put some things in place first, and we'll need some idea of where to go and who can help us get plugged into the relief efforts – but we *can* do something.'

My mind started to spin with all that would need to happen before we could make the trip, but I was confident my colleagues in Ecuador would be more than ready and willing to go and help. Curt and I agreed that relief and development workers would be needed for many months to come, so great was the disaster.

The wheels of administration move slowly in an organization such as ours, especially when something is being proposed that's never been done before. We had to get approval from the mission's leadership, find the funding and assemble a team. It was some weeks later that a group of my colleagues finally set off from Ecuador for south-east Asia. I was still in Britain, so I flew east around the world while they flew west via Los Angeles. We met up at the YWCA in Singapore, where members of our Asia-Pacific team briefed us.

Our final destination was the small Indonesian island of Nias, where one of our partners operated an FM radio station. He also ran an orphanage and this had requested our help. While Nias had not been as badly affected by the tsunami as areas such as the city of Banda Aceh, there had been considerable destruction and yet very little help had come.

The next morning, our team of two nurses and two doctors was joined by a North American colleague who had visited Nias previously and knew our partners there (but who, for her own safety, I'd rather not name) and we headed for Singapore's Changi Airport, where we were to board a plane to Sumatra. We were feeling upbeat, and I couldn't have hoped for a better team. Ian McFarland is a nurse–midwife who has a kind heart and a lovely Northern Ireland accent. He and I had already worked closely with the two doctors in Ecuador, so we all knew each other well.

Steve Nelson is one of the people I admire most in the world. A hard-working missionary doctor with decades of service to the Ecuadorian people, he is a compassionate man who is never too busy or tired to see another patient. He regards his calling as 24/7. He also has a dry sense of humour and his one-liners are legendary. Brad is a brilliant doctor with an amazing mind. He is disciplined, focused and succinct and is the consummate strategic planner – Steve often jokes that he has a thirty-year plan for his life. (In fact, he often jokes that Brad has a thirty-year plan for everyone else as well!)

We landed without mishap in Medan on the island of Sumatra, where we were introduced to our Indonesian partners and a local colleague who was to accompany us as our translator for the next few weeks. It seemed that God had brought together a good, like-minded group of servants to tackle the task ahead – whatever that might turn out to be. I always feel that a good sense of humour and a willingness to adapt are at least as essential as any skills we bring to our work, and on this particular trip 'patience' and 'flexibility' were to become keywords for us.

The next stage of our journey involved a short commercial flight across the Andaman Sea. We were eager to get to work and it was frustrating when we learnt at the airport that the one plane that made the run from Medan to Nias was out of commission. What were we going to do? Our Indonesian friends assured us that other arrangements could be made and before long we were crammed into a propeller aircraft that belonged to the Indonesian air force. There were not enough seats for us all and I suspect that our translator was actually stowed in the cargo hold.

The pilots fired up the engines and started the preflight check. I was sitting directly behind them and I commented on the shoulder patch they had on their jumpsuits. They told me it identified them as 'eyes over the sea'. 'We're pirate-hunters,' they explained. 'We do patrols over the Andaman Sea looking for pirates who steal from the fishermen and board the ferries and seize their cargo.'

After a lot of peering at dials, the pilots embarked on a long discussion about what one particular dial was indicating. The heat in the plane was intense and the temperature seemed to be rising. There was no air-conditioning and we all sat there dripping with sweat. Finally, one of the pilots turned to the other and drew his finger across his throat – which seemed to be the signal to cut the engines. Once the roar of the propellers had died down, the one with the better English turned to us and explained that there was a problem with one of the engines and there was no question of taking off until it was fixed. 'We do not want to die,' he said. We all shared this sentiment, so we climbed out of the plane and went to a local hotel to wait.

The next morning, after a good breakfast of *nasi goreng* (egg fried rice), we were dismayed to learn that the plane was still not fixed and there was no other aircraft that could get us to Nias that day. By now we were getting anxious and frustrated. We had travelled halfway round the world to help the people of Nias and we couldn't make the last few hundred kilometres. 'Lord, what's this all about?' we asked God as we gathered later. We felt we had responded to the island's need prayerfully and obediently and he had opened doors and indicated that we should go there, so it was hard to understand why we couldn't complete the journey. As team leader, I was beginning to feel the pressure – all the time and money we had spent getting to Indonesia and we had yet to see a single patient! I was glad (as I was often to be) that we had Steve with us: his sense of humour could lighten any situation, and his laid-back approach to life brought perspective and peace when I was stressed and fretful.

Our Indonesian translator was also agitated. He wanted to get us to Nias so that we could help his people. 'Is there any other way we can get there?' we asked him. 'Yes,' he said, 'there's a ferry. It crosses every evening and takes twelve hours – but it goes from the other side of Sumatra.' Quick calculations showed that if we could rent a van and leave immediately we might perhaps reach Sibolga, where the ferry docked, in time for that night's sailing.

We scrambled to get our kit together and checked out of the hotel. A van was found and a frantic eight-hour drive across Sumatra east to west ensued. The scenery was breathtaking, the driving even more so as we hurtled down mountainsides and lurched around hairpin bends, bouncing over potholes and dodging goats and chickens and small children. We were amazed to see how similar the country was to the forested areas where we lived in Ecuador. For the final three hours, the excitement was compounded by a torrential storm that swelled the way-side waterfalls until they flooded across the road. I felt anxious for the driver as he peered through a windscreen made opaque by the deluge outside and the condensation inside. I couldn't make out the road ahead, yet he seemed very confident, and not at all bothered by the sheer drop to one side of us. He never took his foot off the accelerator, even as the afternoon drew to a close and the daylight faded – he knew that the clock was against us.

Eventually, we saw lights in the distance – it seemed we were approaching a town. We began to think that perhaps we would make it in time. We raced on through the driving rain until we found ourselves in Sibolga. Then, all of a sudden, the driver slammed on the brakes and the van screeched to a halt. Ahead of us was a long line of stationary traffic. 'What's the hold-up?' Steve asked. He was as unruffled as ever, but we were so close to our goal and it seemed we were going to be frustrated once again. Our translator jumped out of the van, telling us he was going to run ahead to buy our tickets – there was still twenty minutes to go before the ferry was due to sail. Innocently, we hoped and prayed there would still be space for us. In truth, I doubt that an Indonesian ferry is ever 'full'. I know now that they cross the Andaman Sea with as many people and vehicles as need to make the crossing. There is no concept of 'capacity', let alone 'overcrowding'.

After ten minutes or so of inching forward in the queue of traffic, we spotted the translator running back to the van, head down in the rain and soaked to the bone. He looked dejected. 'No ferry,' he told us. What?! Was it full? Were we simply too late? He explained that the ferry we were aiming to catch was broken and there wouldn't be another one for another twenty-four hours. Our shock and disbelief turned to laughter. Who would have believed it? All that crazy driving for nothing! What now? Would we *ever* get to Nias?

But we did get to Nias. We left on the working ferry exactly twenty-four hours later, after a fascinating day in Sibolga where we learnt that all the tall buildings had been constructed with very small holes in their walls, to provide housing for the hundreds of thousands of swallows that make their home in that city. Their nests would later be harvested and sold for $160 a kilo to make bird's-nest soup for the Hong Kong market. We'd never have known *that* if things had gone according to our original plan!

The ferry crossing was smooth, for which we were very grateful. Our translator had bought us 'business-class' tickets, which were very slightly more expensive than the ordinary ones and got us into a smaller communal cabin with about forty other people. It was air-conditioned – supposedly – but, most important, it was non-smoking. We had already gasped our way through far too many meals in smoke-filled restaurants in the few days we had been in Indonesia.

We were each assigned a space on a 'bunk bed' which was actually a cushioned platform. I found myself put between two very nice, well-dressed Indonesian gentlemen and I don't think I would have slept a wink if Ian hadn't volunteered to change places with me. I ended up sleeping soundly next to the North American woman who had come with us from Singapore.

As I drifted off, my mind flitted back over the last couple of days and all the things we had experienced. It seemed surreal to be on an overcrowded ferry in Indonesian waters when only a few days before I had been in the leafy English countryside. Once again, I reassured myself that 'God knows what I'm doing here'. I tried not to think of the pirate-spotters and the fact that their plane was grounded that night as we sailed across the Andaman Sea. Instead, I just committed my way to God as I had done every night, knowing that he was in control wherever we might be – and whatever pirates might be around!

We docked just as the sun was rising. In our 'business-class' accommodation we had been served a cup of coffee, which had set us up nicely for the busy day that lay ahead of us. Indeed, there were many busy days ahead as we set up clinics in homes, schools and churches as well as our partner's orphanage and attended to patients for the next couple of weeks. The devastation the tsunami had caused was evident everywhere, but we were encouraged to see that the people of Nias had a positive spirit and already had salvaged whatever they could and begun to rebuild.

Easter Sunday fell while we were there. We were at the southernmost tip of the island that day and we celebrated our Lord's resurrection on the beach. We prayed for our families and gave thanks for the opportunities God had given us to care for those who had suffered and lost so much. We also praised him for those we had met who loved and followed the resurrected Jesus and were seeking to make him known to others, in the world's most populous Muslim country, often at considerable risk to themselves.

Home seemed very far away that day. I know that the three guys on the team were missing their wives and children. Steve mentioned that he'd taken a GPS reading the night before and at that moment in time, at that very point on the coast of Nias, we were as far away from Ecuador as it was possible to get – literally the other side of the world! Whatever direction we went in from there, we would be moving closer to home.

The three weeks we had planned to spend on the island passed quickly. We were very busy. We enjoyed meeting our Indonesian brothers and sisters from the churches and Brad preached one Sunday. We'd been interviewed on the radio station run by our partner. We loved spending time with the children from the orphanage, and we had treated everyone who came to us for help. One highlight had been visiting a large Muslim family in their home. We spent a long time with them, listening to their account of what had happened the day the waters rose up and hearing of their subsequent struggles and needs. They shared a meal with us, showing incredible generosity at a time of loss and suffering, and before we left they accepted our offer to pray with them for healing and peace.

We left Nias light in heart and spirit, knowing we had done our best and had achieved a great deal. Even so, we all found ourselves doubting the wisdom of such an exhausting trip. It's true that my impulse when I first heard of the tsunami had been: Can I go and help? And certainly my colleagues had been eager to join me. Our partners in Nias had asked us to come, and we had journeyed there believing it was something God wanted us to do. But it was hard not to think that there must have been other medical teams much closer to hand. Had God had something to teach us, perhaps? We discussed our sense of bewilderment at length and came to the conclusion that sometimes we just don't know what God has in mind but it's enough that we should be obedient to his direction.

We flew back to Medan without any problems and debriefed there, expecting to travel to Singapore the next day and then on to our various homes. That night, we were grateful for the welcome of a hotel, a hot shower and a comfortable bed – things our new friends in Nias would not be enjoying for many months to come.

I was woken from a deep sleep by the sounds of splashing water, people running past my door and shouting. I struggled to surface, disoriented. Where was I? For a few seconds I couldn't think, but then it all came back to me. Ah, yes! Sumatra. But something was wrong – it seemed to me the bed was moving. I was suddenly wide awake. After so many years in Ecuador, I knew that the shaking bed, the trembling floor, the swaying walls, could only mean one thing. It was an earthquake – and, I was sure, a big one!

I leapt out of bed and cleared the distance to the door in milliseconds. My room was on the third floor and I opened the door to see streams of people pouring onto the landings and down the stairs. Women were screaming, children were wailing – it was pandemonium. I stumbled my way downstairs with them, staggering into people and falling against the walls. The whole building was swaying and it was very difficult to stay upright and oriented. My heart was racing.

When I reached the car park at the front of the hotel, I clutched at a car to steady myself. The ground was undulating beneath my feet. Unable to keep my balance, I fell to my knees. Then the lights went out. My panic increased. Where was the rest of the team? What actually was happening? Was there going to be another tsunami? Where could I go to be safe? Was there any high ground nearby? I felt alone and very vulnerable as I knelt there in a car park in a strange Muslim country, wearing only a pair of sleeping shorts and a tee shirt.

The quake – and the attendant chaos – seemed to go on for a long time. Finally, through the darkness, I spotted Ian. Ian is tall and has a distinctive way of standing, with his legs apart and his hands in the back pockets of his jeans. I only saw his silhouette but I knew it was him. I ran over to him and we hugged each other in relief. I was so happy to see him!

'Where's your stuff?' he asked me. Stuff? 'Your passport and your valuables.' He indicated the small backpack he was carrying. In my desperation to escape from the hotel, I had left all my things in my unlocked room. At that moment I still didn't care about my passport – I just wanted to find the rest of the team! Ian suggested we should go back inside to look for Steve and Brad, but also so that I could get dressed and retrieve my things. I was too scared to go back in. Ian said he would go for me, but like a little child I didn't want to be left on my own again. So we waited outside, looking around vainly for our colleagues.

The lights came back on after half an hour or so. People began to drift back into the hotel, wading through the lobby, which had been flooded when the earthquake created waves in the swimming pool. I got dressed and collected my things and we went to find Steve and Brad.

12

The House of Infidels

It still amazes me that Steve and Brad didn't even get out of bed during the second-biggest earthquake ever recorded in Indonesia. We found them in their hotel room, still curled up under the blankets. We didn't know at the time how severe the quake was, but today we joke that they don't get up for anything less than 8.8 on the Richter scale. In fact, that earthquake was one of the ten most powerful worldwide since 1900!

We turned on the television to see what was being reported, but we could find nothing. Concluding that the shaking must just have felt worse where we were – and certainly hoping that was the case – Ian and I returned to our rooms and tried to get back to sleep.

Around 4 a.m. a loud hammering woke me and sent my heart into overdrive again. I leapt out of bed – this time, already fully clothed – and rushed to open the door, to be greeted by Ian's anxious face. He told me we needed to meet the others immediately in Brad's room. Nias had been hit hard by the quake. Our partner there had called to say that the radio station and the orphanage had been destroyed. There was a lot of damage across the island and he feared that many people were dead or injured. Could we please go back there to help?

We stopped to pray in that moment for our friends on the island. We prayed for the children at the orphanage, for the pastors, for the people we had met and treated. We prayed for wisdom in our decisions. We asked God to show us what to do.

We resolved to try to get back to Nias as soon as day broke. Mindful of how difficult it had been to get there the first time round, we wondered how we were going to manage it. I succeeded in getting a call through to Quito and the secretary who answered the phone broke down in tears of relief when she heard we were safe. Reports of the earthquake had already reached our colleagues in Ecuador through the news services our radio station subscribes to and, knowing we had been in Nias, they had feared the worst. They had just gathered for prayer as my phone call came in – God knew that they and our families needed reassurance! It was the only international call we were able to make, as cellphone services failed soon after.

As the dawn arrived, we were still glued to the television in Brad's room. Images from Banda Aceh in northern Indonesia filled the screen. People were abandoning their homes in panic, fleeing on bicycles or on foot, terrified that another tsunami was imminent. Clutching all the possessions they could carry, holding babies close to them, dragging crying toddlers behind them, they were desperately seeking the safety of high ground. Their fear was almost tangible. Police with megaphones were urging them to stay calm and go back to their homes, assuring them that there would not be another tsunami. Still the people fled.

Our Indonesian friend and interpreter who had been with us throughout the trip was busy trying to make contact with other non-government agencies that might have chartered planes or helicopters, to arrange for us to fly to Nias as soon as possible. We packed our bags hastily and left for the airport as soon as we could. Perhaps we would be able to get on some kind of emergency flight. We soon learnt that there would not be any commercial flights to Nias for a long time – the runway there was severely damaged. What could we do?

Then we heard that some smaller planes might be making the trip, if enough of the runway was still intact for them to land on. It sounded dangerous to me. Groups of people were standing around hoping to get on a flight. Most of them appeared to be journalists – film crews and reporters always seem to find a way to get to the 'action'. Surely, I thought, they would let the medical teams go first? Unfortunately not.

As we waited, we got talking to others. We saw someone wearing a hat with the MAF logo on it and we introduced ourselves. We told him we worked closely with MAF in the Oriente, where for many years its pilots had airlifted medical emergency cases to our hospital in Shell. At the mention of Shell, a young woman in a Samaritan's Purse polo shirt turned and looked at us. 'I grew up in Shell!' she exclaimed. 'My dad was a surgeon at the hospital there.' Steve had spent many years in Shell and when she told us her name, he said he knew her father well. She stared at him for a few moments and then flung her arms around him. 'Uncle Steve!' she cried. It turned out that as a girl she had run around in the forest with his children. The mission world is a small one!

A second man from MAF observed that his brother had also worked in Shell, as a mechanic with the Fellowship – and we soon established that we knew him, too! Thus it was that around midday Brad and Steve got onto the first MAF flight to Nias, with the understanding that Ian and I would soon follow. The pilot wasn't sure that the state of the runway there would allow him to land and then take off again, so the plan was to go in with a light load and take a look.

As I watched the small red-and-white plane climbing into the sky, my heart was gripped by anxiety. The responsibility I felt as team leader weighed heavily on me. I knew that ideally teams should stay together, not split up. Brad and Steve were heading off into the unknown without any means of direct communication or any contingency plan of action if I didn't hear back from them. I wondered where they would end up and how we would find them again. What if the plane came to harm as it tried to land? Ian and I settled down to pray and wait.

The afternoon wore on and as evening drew on it became clear that he and I would be going nowhere that day. Word finally reached us that the plane had managed to land on a small remnant of runway and that Brad and Steve were OK. Ian and I were to go out on the first flight the next day, so we went back to the hotel to make the most of its hot showers, hot food and soft beds while we could.

Early the next morning, as I gazed out of the window of the Cessna at the mirror-like surface of the Andaman Sea, I found it hard to believe that anything untoward could have happened. There was no hint of the death and destruction that had been visited on the island of Nias just a few miles to the west. When the plane went into a steep descent, it was as if we were swooping out of the clouds like a bird.

A few minutes later, we touched down – hard. The plane bounced along for a few hundred metres and our harnesses held us tight as the pilot stamped on the brakes. By the time we had stopped moving, we were at the very end of what was left intact of the runway. As we climbed out, a motorcycle drew up alongside us with Brad on the back. Two more motorbikes arrived, with empty pillions for Ian and me. Brad explained that the roads were so badly damaged, blocked by landslides, fallen trees and rubble, that this was the only way to get around.

Clutching our suitcases in front of us, we hung on for dear life as we sped off to the ruin that used to be Gunungsitoli, the principal city of Nias.

Our first stop was the hospital, where we met up with Steve. It was a huge relief to be reunited with him and Brad again, even though we had been apart for only a matter of hours. The greatest tragedy, the greatest danger is tempered when you face it with close friends – and we were already close friends, and were to become much closer as the days unfolded and we witnessed together some unspeakably sad situations. There is something therapeutic in being able to discuss with others experiences you have shared. Different people process things differently, but at the end of this trip the four of us all agreed that we had had sufficient time together to work through our feelings and come to terms in a healthy way with what we had witnessed.

Brad and Steve did their best to orient us to what was happening. There were huge cracks in the walls of the hospital and some of them appeared to be leaning, but there was a part of the building that seemed to be more or less safe. The patients who had already been in the hospital were receiving care from the regular staff (or, at least, those who had shown up that day). There were no Indonesian doctors on site, and few nurses. Some personnel from the French Red Cross were out in the city searching for survivors in the wreckage. And that was it. At that point, the four of us were the only disaster-relief workers in the hospital.

Steve showed me into a room where a number of women were lying, on beds or gurneys or even on the floor. They still had on the filthy clothes they had been wearing when they were pulled from the rubble. The floor was dirty and there was blood and flies were everywhere. The heat was already overpowering, and the stench of sweat and urine seemed to add to the sense of chaos. Women were wailing, in pain, in distress, in fear. Family members wandered in in a daze, looking for their loved ones or just staring, with eyes full of tears. It was a shocking scene.

Above the din, Steve pointed out four women. 'These need to be evacuated first, Sheila,' he said. I felt dazed. 'OK,' I replied. 'So, how do we do this? When will the ambulance get here? Where will they go?' He explained that they were trying to find somewhere to land the helicopters that would take the patients to the airport, since the roads were impassable. Once a suitable place had been found, the patients would be carried there to await evacuation. He didn't know where they would be taken to. Then he left.

I stood and stared at the devastation around me. I stared at the faces of these women. I will never forget them. I looked at their broken limbs sticking out at all angles. I recoiled as I saw their crushed arms and legs, the gashes on their heads, the open wounds on their faces where the flies were already beginning to gather – the women didn't even have the strength to brush them off. I saw the looks on their faces: of disbelief, of shock, of pain, of fear, of anguish. I felt as helpless as they were. I didn't know what to do, where to start. 'Lord, help me!' I prayed. 'Help me to know who to help first and what to do!'

As I have recounted this story over the years, I've always been embarrassed to say what I did next. I walked out of the room, found a mop and some water and disinfectant and came back and cleaned the floor.

That simple process of doing something practical, something familiar, something I could cope with gave me the space to breathe and think. In reality, the floor did not stay clean for long, but it smelt cleaner and looked better, and as I worked I began to think logically. My training came back to me. I was a nurse. I knew what to do: assess, plan, implement and evaluate.

I identified the most gravely injured woman and began to examine her from head to toe. I checked her 'vital signs' – her blood pressure, pulse and breathing rate – and recorded them. I bathed her wounds and bandaged her limbs, I assessed her level of consciousness, I found some painkiller and administered it. I tried to establish what had happened to her and which parts of her were injured and which hurt most. I found clean linen for her bed. I soothed her and tried, in English words, to convey my love and concern for her.

An Australian journalist wandered in and when I heard her speaking Indonesian I grabbed her and insisted that she ask the patients their names. She wrote them on strips of paper from her notebook and we taped them to the women's clothes along with details of any medicine I had given them, observations about their level of consciousness and a note of their vital signs. She stayed by my side as I worked all that day. We worked our way methodically around the room, trying to give care, trying to bring comfort. When any patient seemed to be deteriorating, one of us rushed to find Brad or Steve, who were just as busy and overstretched attending to the men and children.

By the afternoon, the evacuation of the patients had begun, but no sooner had one been stretchered out than someone else took their place. Throughout the day, powerful aftershocks shook the unstable building and we were often sent outside by the police and military, who had arrived at the hospital to establish some kind of order and also act as porters. It felt very wrong to leave that room knowing that those left inside had no choice but to lie there helplessly and hope and pray that the walls would remain standing.

Day turned to night and the evacuation flights were halted. Our team was ordered to take a break and Indonesian nurses from the hospital began to show up to help. One of the local pastors took us to his home and found us all somewhere to sleep. As I was the only female in the team, I had a room to myself at the very back of the house. I was grateful to be spared Ian's infamous high-decibel snoring and yet I hated being alone. The aftershocks were still going on and everything feels worse in the dark. I was sure that the house would collapse and bury us and persuaded myself that I needed to stay awake to warn the guys and get them outside if there was another big quake. Eventually – I think, through sheer exhaustion – I, too, slept.

In any major disaster, relief begins to arrive fairly quickly and Nias was no exception. Many aid agencies still had personnel based in Aceh working through the aftermath of the tsunami. Soon, aid workers began to trickle and then flood onto the island. The Indonesian military took over the hospital within a couple of days and declared that most of the buildings were unsafe. The World Food Programme anchored a ship offshore and began to distribute food. The United Nations started to co-ordinate efforts to treat injuries, prevent disease and secure supplies of food and water. Every day, Brad attended their team meetings and fed the latest news back, including any data that might presage the outbreak of some epidemic – and the death toll.

At one of these meetings, he bumped into our friend from Samaritan's Purse again. Now that the hospital was being run by the military, we had been wondering what we should do. She told Brad that there were many areas outside the cities where all communication was down and nobody knew what the situation was. She asked how flexible we were. 'On a scale of one to ten, with ten being the most flexible, I would say we are twelve,' he joked. She asked if we would be willing to be taken by helicopter to some of the more remote parts of the island. Of course the answer was yes.

Next morning, we showed up at the appointed place, loaded down with water and ramen noodles (to sustain us over the next few days) and medical supplies. We split into two teams: Ian and Brad, and Steve and me.

It was to be the first helicopter ride of my life. I am an anomaly in my family because I've never been particularly fond of flying – indeed, I almost have a phobia about it. Both my parents loved to fly. One of my brothers is a commercial pilot and another one used to fly microlights. Nowadays, I can get on a plane without too much problem, though I still have to pray really hard. In those days, it was worse.

Climbing into the small helicopter, I was comforted to learn that the man at the controls was hugely experienced – he was a Vietnam war veteran whose regular job now was as pilot to the famous evangelist, Billy Graham. He certainly inspired confidence! We prayed before we lifted off, and as we swung up into the sky I found myself actually enjoying the sensation, which is very different from 'normal' flying.

As we flew low over the island, we began to appreciate the enormity of what had happened. Whole communities were totally destroyed. Houses lay in ruins. Groups of people, hearing the sound of our rotors, would gather, waving and signalling desperately for us to land, to bring aid to them. I vividly remember the smells that wafted up to us in the helicopter – the smells of death and decay – as we flew over piles of rubble in which men, women and children lay buried. Their homes had become their tombs, and their tombs stank.

Our pilot had been given clear instructions about which communities we were to visit, but it was difficult to distinguish one place from another as every landmark had gone. The topography of the island seemed to have changed completely. On one occasion, we landed on the edge of what appeared to be a swamp. People were standing there ready to receive the help they'd been waiting for, but our pilot soon realized we were not in the right place and within a few moments we had taken to the skies again. My heart almost broke in pieces when I saw the looks of disillusionment and despair. 'Why can't you stay?' they asked us. They told us there were many injured in their village and they were desperate for help and supplies. Our pilot promised to tell the authorities of their need and said that he hoped to come back.

Our intended destination that day was very close to the epicentre of the quake. We were to be the first relief workers on the ground and our job was to assess the situation, treat as many of the injured as we could and identify those who needed to be evacuated when the helicopter returned. When we landed, we jumped out of the aircraft to be met by a group of beautiful Indonesian nuns, dressed in spotless white – a surreal contrast to the scene of destruction and decay all around us. They ushered us over to some motorcycles and we were whisked up a hill above the town to their convent, where they showed us into a large hall full of people waiting to be attended to. We could see we were going to be busy for a long time. I asked for boiling water and the nuns ran to fetch it, thinking we required it to wash our hands. In fact, we needed coffee! Both Steve and I are coffee addicts and we work much better once we have had our daily fix of caffeine. Our hosts looked on in astonishment as we made a couple of cups of instant, and then we set to work.

I'm not a doctor, I'm a nurse. There have been times, however, when I've been obliged to do things that would have been far better handled by someone with more knowledge, training and skills than me – and this was one of them. We set up a few benches and managed to create a couple of makeshift 'consulting rooms'. I was glad that Steve was close by as I set to work triaging and dealing with whatever I could before referring each patient to him. We blessed God when a well-dressed young Indonesian man who spoke almost perfect English showed up to help with translation. We later learnt that he was a very successful businessman from Jakarta, the capital of Indonesia, who'd made his way to this remote place to check on his elderly parents after he heard reports of the first earthquake and the tsunami. He stayed with us and interpreted for us the whole time we were there. For sure, he was God's provision for us. (His parents, I should add, turned out to be alive and well, though the ruin of the harbour spelt the end of their business trading in rubber.)

We worked long hours. We were the only medical help to have arrived and the line of people needing attention and treatment never seemed to get any shorter. The beautiful nuns ran here and there and tried to find everything we needed. They were the embodiment of kindness to us and our patients, dispensing love and medicine to all.

Late that afternoon, Steve called me to one side. 'Sheila,' he said, 'there's a gal here who, by the sound of it, had a miscarriage on the night of the earthquake. She's still bleeding and if we don't stop it she'll die.' I looked across at his 'consulting room' and saw a young Muslim woman, completely covered up, sitting on a stool. From her posture, I could tell that she was weak and finding it hard even to stay upright. She had already been losing blood for several days and I wondered how much she had lost and how she could even sit up unsupported. What could we do? Steve explained that if we could manage to remove the piece of placenta that undoubtedly was still inside her womb, the bleeding would stop and she would probably recover with the help of antibiotics. 'What surgical instruments have we got with us?' he asked. 'I need something I can use to grab hold of that bit of tissue and remove it.'

Casting my mind's eye over our supplies, I said that the only thing we had that might conceivably serve his purpose was a needle driver from a basic suture kit. This has a long shaft with a clamp at the end that we use to hold the needle when we are sewing up wounds. Steve thought he could make it work. 'What do we have to sterilize it?' he enquired. I suggested asking the nuns to boil some more water, but the light was already fading and Steve didn't think there was time. We decided to clean the driver as thoroughly as we could with alcohol hand rub. It was the best we could do.

We asked the nuns to get everyone out of the room to protect the woman's privacy. They closed the shutters on the windows and guarded the doors so that no one could wander in. Steve put on his surgical gloves; I readied the instruments, such as they were, and stood beside the woman, holding her hand. I had a blood-pressure cuff at the ready to monitor her vital signs.

The principal danger was a catastrophic haemorrhage. Normally, such a procedure would be done under general anaesthetic in a clean operating theatre with blood replacement products, intravenous fluids and clotting aids to hand, but we didn't have any of those luxuries. We prayed and put our trust in God.

It seemed as if hours passed as I watched Steve working. The woman clung on to me and covered her face with her other hand, groaning quietly. It must have been very painful and yet she remained stoical. At last, Steve drew out the needle driver with the offending piece of tissue in its jaws. Together, we breathed a sigh of relief and offered up silent prayers of thanksgiving.

However, within minutes our patient started bleeding profusely. Steve appeared to remain completely calm as he applied internal pressure, but I was fighting back feelings of panic and trying not to betray how anxious I was. I began to question myself: What on earth had possessed us to undertake a procedure like this when we were so ill-equipped? I was anxious to save her, but anxious also about our own safety. How would the Muslim community react if she died? My mind began to run riot imagining what might happen. 'God, please help us!' I prayed. 'Make the bleeding stop! Save her life, please!'

I checked the woman's blood pressure and saw how low it had dropped. She was losing a lot of blood. Steve and I spoke English words of encouragement to her as we monitored her pulse. She was pale, her breathing was rapid, her heart rate had increased – all signs of the onset of hypovolemic shock. Steve remained calm, however, and continued to apply internal pressure as we quietly discussed what we could do. Our patient desperately needed to take in fluid if she was to survive. We asked the nuns to prepare some oral rehydration fluid and we urged the woman to drink it. By now she was barely conscious, but with our help she drank a litre. And then another. I noticed her blood pressure stabilize, then start to creep up. I began to sweat less and breathe more easily – and, more important, so did she. Had she stopped bleeding? Would she pull through?

After ten agonizing minutes or so, it seemed that the answer was yes. In fact, her recovery progressed rapidly. Within half an hour, she wanted to leave the convent! 'I cannot stay in the house of infidels,' she insisted. 'I must go.' We persuaded one of the young novices to donate some clean underwear to her and then we helped her to her feet and escorted her to the door. Before she left, Steve gave her a big hug. I told him he probably shouldn't be hugging a Muslim woman – but on reflection we agreed that, in the light of what had happened, and not least the nature of his surgical intervention, a hug wasn't exactly a big deal!

Later as we debriefed, Steve confessed that he had been very worried. At one point, he said, he couldn't even get a pulse. She had almost died. I have to record that God worked a miracle through him.

We went back to the main convent house that night for a delicious and most welcome meal. There, we met a British journalist who had arrived by boat that day. He told us he had come into the room where we were seeing our patients but, as we were so busy, he hadn't wanted to interrupt. He said he had come to that place to get as close as he could to the epicentre of the earthquake. He planned to report how the harbour had been lifted by the huge forces the quake had released, so that the sea was now almost 200 metres away. He interviewed Steve briefly and then lent him his satellite phone so he could call his family and tell them where we were.

He left at daybreak on the first boat out to get his exclusive story filed. We later learnt that he had written about Steve and me in the *Guardian*. For some of my friends in Britain, it was the first news they had had that we were alive and well and working hard!

The helicopter returned a few days later. We placed our most severely injured patients on board on stretchers and climbed in with them. Almost all of them were facing amputation of one or more limbs. Their pain and weariness were etched on their faces and their eyes were filled with fear. Where were they being taken? How would their families know? What would happen to them? Would they ever see their homes again? We prayed for them and with them and, as we rose above the island, my heart felt broken. I gulped in air, trying to hold myself together, not wanting to break down and bawl. How much these people had suffered! How much they had lost!

As we landed in Sibolga, Steve and I looked forward to reconnecting with Ian and Brad. Our pilot had told us that the military would be flying them up from the south of the island where they had been working. When we disembarked, we noticed that people were scurrying around with concern written all over their faces. It wasn't long before we heard that a helicopter had gone down and everyone on board was dead. Immediately our thoughts turned to our colleagues. We couldn't even put our fears into words.

Later, we learnt that it was a group of Australian aid workers who had been killed. We couldn't help feeling immense relief that Ian and Brad were safe, and yet we grieved for the families and friends of those who had died. Somehow, it made the magnitude of the suffering of the Indonesian people more real to us.

Our final departure from Nias involved hanging around the airport until we could find someone willing to fly us to Medan. Over the hours of waiting we talked through all that had happened over the past week. Only then did things make sense. The initial hold-ups and delays in our arrival on the island now seemed clearly to be God's perfect timing. He had planned to use us far more extensively than we could ever have imagined. For such a time as this (as it says in Esther 4:14) he had put us in that place. It was humbling to see how he had orchestrated everything so that we would be exactly where he wanted us to be for his purposes.

Once our flight out was arranged, everything followed quickly. Within an hour of leaving Nias we were in Medan and from there we were able to get a commercial flight to Singapore almost immediately. Hours after leaving behind us the tragedy of Nias we were sitting in Starbucks drinking coffee. It was unreal. I found it hard – no, impossible – to reconcile everything I had seen, smelt and felt with my present surroundings. I asked myself whether it had all really happened, or had I just woken up from a horrible nightmare? The stench of death on my (soon to be discarded) clothes confirmed the truth. It had indeed really happened.

13

No Pills for Broken Hearts

In October 2005, an e-mail came out of the blue. I knew there had been a huge earthquake in central Pakistan but I didn't know anyone living or working in the devastated area. So, when the message arrived in my inbox, I was taken aback. Pakistan? Really?

A partner organization was faced with a crisis. The earthquake had caused massive destruction and loss of life and left hundreds of thousands of people injured. Our partners had no medical personnel in-country and, overwhelmed by the suffering and loss, were appealing for help. Could we send a medical team? This is the kind of challenge I love. Could we? Yes. So, would we? Maybe. There were a hundred questions in my mind: What skills were needed? How would we get visas? Who would interpret for us? Not the least of my concerns was whether anyone would actually volunteer to go. Who in their right mind would travel almost halfway around the globe to care for people from a culture so different from that of Ecuador?

Within a couple of days, God provided answers to all my questions. Yes, we had staff who were willing – in fact, eager – to go. We would send a team of five doctors, a nurse and a children's worker. They would travel to Islamabad via London and would join others already there on the ground to provide surgical trauma care and general medicine to people affected by the quake. Pakistan's honorary consul in Ecuador would issue visas and our partners in Pakistan would provide logistics and interpreters. Amazingly, things came together quickly and within a few days our staff in Quito gathered round to pray with those who were going. For the first time, Ecuadorians from our hospitals in Quito and Shell were to be part of our disaster-response team.

That first team arrived in Pakistan within days of the earthquake and immediately set to work operating in various different venues, including a (literally) inflatable Japanese hospital which had been quickly assembled and equipped. Both the orthopaedic surgeons and the anaesthetist were much in demand, and the children's worker was able to comfort and entertain the children as they endured frightening and some-times painful procedures. Some members of the team were sent up-country to other areas affected by the quake – we later learnt that some of them were serving within a few hundred yards of the compound where Osama bin Laden was holed up!

We then received word that a follow-up team was needed. Once again, we started to look for suitable volunteers. We heard that a plastic surgeon would be helpful, as well as an anaesthetist, some GPs – at least one of them a woman – and nurses. Once again, Ecuadorians stepped forward. One of our plastic surgeons – my dear friend Guadeloupe Santamaria – an anaesthetist, Alberto Corral, and a female GP, Ximena Pozo, agreed to go with a 'family practitioner' from the USA and two British nurses, including me.

We landed in Islamabad early in the morning. As we disembarked from the plane, we had to find our way through the mountains of food, tents and medical supplies piled up around the airport. The three women in our party covered our heads as best we could with the scarves we had brought for the purpose, though we found it a constant struggle to make sure that our hair didn't peek out! In our pre-trip orientation to the local culture, we had learnt about the importance of head coverings for women, and had also been told that women are expected not to make eye contact with men, let alone greet them unless a handshake is offered. We tried to remember all these things as we shuffled, heads bowed, into the terminal. We were very conscious of the fact that Pakistan is an Islamic country and we were anxious to be culturally sensitive and respectful in the way we dressed and behaved.

Things were much easier for the three men on our team. As we were ushered into immigration to get our papers processed, they were invited to sit while we women stood in a huddle in a corner, essentially ignored. I began to see that my role for the next few weeks would be to try to make myself as invisible as possible. For such a strong-minded person as me, this was going to be a challenge!

Our partners had sent someone to meet us with a young Pakistani driver and forty-five minutes later we were heading out into the city of Islamabad. I was surprised to see that the part we travelled through had wide streets, gardens and trees. It was a pleasant surprise – for some reason I had expected it to be a drab grey! We could see no evidence of the earthquake at all. Evidently, Islamabad had not been affected.

There was a lot of waiting around over the next few days as our partners tried to figure out where we could best be deployed. Eventually, we were told that the greatest needs were in some of the more remote areas of Kashmir, where there are communities living high up in the mountains. Many of their homes had been destroyed completely and thousands of people were now living in tents. Neither medical help nor emergency supplies of food had yet reached them, as a result of the landslides that followed the earthquake, and with winter closing in fast the situation was becoming desperate.

It was clear to us that we could assist in those areas. We had many years' experience of running mobile clinics in the mountains and rainforests of Ecuador. Our doctors were used to relying on their own diagnostic skills and prescribing from just a small formulary of medicines. We were keen walkers and climbers and we relished the thought of getting up into the mountains, while the idea of living in tents didn't faze us at all. But what to do with the surgeon and the anaesthetist? They couldn't work without an operating theatre. We were told that their skills were badly needed in a Christian hospital in the far east of the country, on the border with Afghanistan. The area was volatile, however, and they would have to be taken in by a military escort.

As we met together to discuss these options, I was moved to hear Guadeloupe say with conviction: 'I will go wherever I am needed most and God can use me.' She had been told by the Pakistani consul in Quito that she and Ximena might be the first two Ecuadorian women ever to visit his country – certainly he had never issued a visa to one before! She was willing to do all she could to care for those who needed her skills and to bring God's love to the furthest reaches of Pakistan without any thought for her own safety.

She and Alberto, the anaesthetist, packed for the journey and we gathered round and laid hands on them and prayed that God would protect them and bless their work. We wept as they left and I wondered whether we had been right to send them. Would we ever see them again?

The next day, three more of us set off for the mountains: nurse–midwife Ian from Northern Ireland, Ximena and me. Jeff Maudlin, the US doctor, had already gone on ahead and we were following in a beaten-up van, along with a volunteer French firefighter called Jérémie who had turned up from somewhere, a driver and someone I think was supposed to be an interpreter. We had no idea where we were going and no means of communication and were just trusting that we were in good hands. In fact, as we reminded ourselves often, we were in God's hands.

The city soon gave way to countryside and now we could see all around us evidence of the destruction the earthquake had caused. Houses and shops lay in ruins. People were sleeping in tents and makeshift shelters and there were long queues for water, food and blankets. Eventually, we turned off the main 'highway' (which was actually one of the historic 'silk roads' running from China through Pakistan to the Mediterranean) onto a gravel track. Our ancient vehicle began to climb higher into the mountains, its engine straining as it struggled up the steep gradient and lurched around hairpin bends. As darkness fell, we wondered where exactly we were heading for and how much further it was. We also began to question the wisdom of travelling at night on such isolated roads in that turbulent country. In the mountains of Pakistan, the night truly is black!

Abruptly, lights appeared ahead of us and the van juddered to a halt. There was loud shouting and we were surrounded by men. Our driver and the interpreter jumped out and, without a word to us, disappeared into the darkness. We sat in silence, very frightened, fearing the worst. What was happening? Were we about to be kidnapped? Or killed?

After what seemed to us an age but was maybe ten minutes, someone strode up to the van and shone a powerful torch around its interior, illuminating us women, with our heads covered and bowed, and the two remaining men. Then, three men climbed in. They were dressed like soldiers and were carrying guns. My heart was beating wildly when, unexpectedly, a voice broke the silence speaking impeccable English. 'Good evening, and welcome to Pakistan. Thank you for coming to help. This area is not too safe, so we are sending some soldiers to escort you. Your doctor is already at the camp and you will join him soon. Would any of you care for a cup of tea?' I almost laughed out loud at this courteous offer. A strange touch of British hospitality in the most unlikely circumstance! We were soon on our way again with lightened hearts.

Our destination turned out to be a valley with a river rushing through it and beautiful mountains all around, one of which was called Moses' Carpet because it was always covered with a layer of snow. We were being hosted in an army encampment, in a small village called Manda Gucha, where tents had been provided for us. It was very cold. When we arrived, we were given chai and some spicy food and then introduced to the captain who was in charge of the camp. His name was Imran and he seemed very young, but he spoke English fluently and treated us with unfailing kindness and consideration. Throughout our stay in the camp, we had hot water to bathe in, a latrine tent was kept clean for the women's exclusive use and there was even a special meal with Coca-Cola on America's Thanksgiving Day, which fell while we were there. At all times, we were shown the utmost respect.

Our bodyguard was called Malik and everywhere Ximena and I went, he and his AK47 went with us. I don't know what danger we may have been in, but he looked out for us constantly. I suspect his heart sank every time we decided to go for a walk round the village, since he always had to come with us. On many occasions on these walks we were invited to take chai with the local people.

On our very first day, we woke up to the sound of the Muslim call to prayer. The intense cold made it hard to get out of our sleeping bags, and when we eventually emerged we were treated to a meal of spicy potatoes swimming in oil with flat bread.

H'mm! We were also offered hot tea, which went down rather better. We could already see our female patients squatting in an orderly line, their children around them, outside the tent that would serve as our consulting room. When I say we could see them, I mean we could see the outline of their bodies – they were swathed in black, with their faces completely covered. Jeff and Ian had also been assigned a tent to work in and there too was a line of squatting men.

An interpreter was provided for us and we set to work. It very soon became apparent that most of these women had never received any medical attention, either before the earthquake or since. Women's health care seemed very deficient in that remote valley. As each patient entered our tent, she would remove her veil and only then could we see her as an individual. There were old women with wizened faces, teenagers with large eyes and shy smiles, and beautiful young women with small children clinging to them. Many of them complained of the same symptoms: 'I have pain in my whole body. Everything hurts. I cannot sleep. My heart is beating very fast. I find myself crying all the time.'

What could we say?

> Your body hurts because you were battered and bruised when your house fell down on top of you. We can help you with that. We can set your bones and bandage your wounds and we have pills to relieve the pain.
>
> You can't sleep because you are anxious and afraid, because the ground continues to shake. We have pills that will help you sleep, and help you get back into the pattern of sleeping.
>
> Your heart is beating very fast because you're suffering from post-traumatic stress and you're having panic attacks. And yes, we have pills for that, too.

But you are crying all the time because your heart is broken. When the school collapsed that day, you lost three children. When their small bodies were pulled out from under a mountain of rubble, you saw the fear on their beautiful, lifeless faces. You can't forget that awful moment, and you can't forgive yourself for not being there in time to save them. We do not have pills for broken hearts.

What could we do or say to ease their suffering? Nothing – except listen to their stories, share their fears, put our arms around them and weep with them for what they had lost. And we would tell them, 'We know the God who has promised to "bind up the broken-hearted" [Ps. 147:3] and we will ask him to bring comfort and healing to your heart', and we would offer to pray with them.

It still amazes me that, with very few exceptions, these Muslim women accepted that offer almost with gratitude. We would pray in English and our interpreter would translate for them. I've been asked many times how we knew that she translated what we actually said; but we were not praying to the interpreter and God understands English!

Our days fell into a kind of routine. Woken early every morning by the call to prayer, we would drag ourselves from our snug cocoons and eat breakfast. We worked hard, seeing as many patients as we could while there was still daylight – there was no electricity in the camp. By now, the first snows had begun to fall, and so after supper we would get back into our sleeping bags to keep warm. Fortunately, Ximena and I were already very close friends, because as the only women in the camp we were together 24/7.

Sometimes in the evenings, the soldiers would make a fire out in the open and our team would be invited to gather round it with them to keep warm. At times, I think they forgot there were two foreign women among them and they would sing and dance together. As we sat huddled up on the snow under the stars, I marvelled that I could be there so far from my home and family and yet so privileged to experience life in a Pakistani military camp high up in Kashmir! How many women from Solihull ever get to do that?

As well as serving in the village of Manda Gucha, we spent several days hiking way up the valley, beyond the end of the road. Besides our ubiquitous bodyguard, three or four soldiers accompanied us as guides and porters. We reached a place called Sachan, which was so isolated and so rugged that it seemed to me almost uninhabitable. Certainly, the bleakness of the mountains towering above it made it feel very inhospitable and far away from anything we would call 'civilization'. We were probably the first Christians, as well as the first medics, ever to walk those trails.

The people streamed down from the mountains and came from far afield to get medical attention in Sachan. In fact, the area turned out to be quite populous. Some of their injuries were distressing. One woman with a spinal fracture had received no care even a month after the earthquake. We saw head injuries, fractured limbs, cuts, contusions and wounds, and everywhere suffering, sorrow and hopeless resignation in people's eyes. How desperate and sad these women's lives seemed to me! I found myself weeping for them. My mind was full of questions to God as I contemplated the contrast between my life and theirs. 'Why wasn't I born in Pakistan, Lord? Why has my life been so privileged? Why does life seem so unfair?' I received no answers. As I reflected on these things, it made me recognize and be thankful for all the blessings God had showered upon me. There, high up in Pakistani Kashmir, I renewed my commitment to God, to live my life for others and to serve him.

It was hard work to keep our own morale high. The little we could do didn't seem to be of any significance in the face of such loss and need. 'How do you cope with all that suffering?' I have been asked many times, and 'How can you help everyone?' The answer is that I know I can't help everyone, but I can comfort *that* weeping woman in front of me, I can bring relief to *that* feverish child, I do have medicine for *that* elderly woman who comes to me with stiff, sore joints. These are the people I *can* help – the people God puts before me. More important, I can pray and offer my work as worship to God and bring him into each situation in an incarnational way. He lives in his people and we take his presence with us wherever we go. He is the only one who brings relief and gives healing and peace. We are merely channels for his love.

After three weeks in Pakistan, I had to leave, to attend some meetings arranged earlier in Delhi. The rest of my team were staying on for a while longer, so I travelled back to Islamabad by local transportation, a battered old minivan. Jérémie, the French firefighter, came too, along with what seemed like a hundred Pakistani men and women. As we hurtled down the mountain, I was sure we were going to die. The van's brakes seemed ineffectual and the driving was very fast.

Every now and again, a voice from the back of the van would call out in English: 'Jérémie, this is a very dangerous place! The whole mountain fell down. There are thirty people still buried here.' A little further on, it was: 'Jérémie, a whole bus full of people went off the road here. Many dead.' Then: 'Jérémie, a landslide swept away twenty people right here. Very dangerous!' The speaker, who never identified himself, had been sent by the army to make sure that Jérémie and I got to Islamabad safely, but he did nothing to put us at our ease.

Once, in the middle of a heavy downpour, mud and stones began to stream down the mountainside onto the road, which was particularly narrow at that point. We were literally driving on the edge. At any moment, I thought, we would be swept off the road into the canyon hundreds of feet below. The driver's mate, a skinny man with a mournful face, got out of the vehicle, rolled up his baggy trousers to his knees, hitched up his long shirt and ran barefoot in front of us for a couple of miles, watching for falling rocks. Many times he would signal us to stop and wait, and then call out when all was clear. Our driver peered anxiously up at the mountain and accelerated hard, bouncing his passengers around like popcorn. We were all terrified. The others began to say, in unison, '*Allahu akbar . . .*' I knew that God was great, but I still couldn't help thinking: I'm going to die!

But we didn't die. We made it back to Islamabad. Later, so did the rest of the team. Guadeloupe and Alberto had many stories to tell of their adventures at the hospital and the things they had seen and done. They told us of the patients they had treated, the operations they had performed and the ways in which they, too, had seen the hand of God helping them in their work. Guadeloupe especially, as a mother herself, had been touched by the plight of the women and children in particular.

We left Pakistan different people from the ones who had arrived just a few weeks earlier. What we had experienced had changed us on many levels, but each of us felt certain that God still had work for us to do in service to him around the world.

I flew out of Islamabad on Pakistan International Airlines. It was my first flight in this part of the world as an 'unaccompanied woman' and it meant I had to queue for a separate security check. It also meant that I couldn't get served at the airport restaurant. No matter how I tried to get the (male) waiters' attention, they all ignored me! Hungry and grumpy, I finally boarded my flight to Delhi, only to find I was seated next to a large man in flowing white robes, whose red-dyed beard told me he had completed the hajj. I was actually a bit afraid of him – perhaps he was one of the mujahidin? I carefully avoided eye contact, made sure that not one square millimetre of me was touching one square millimetre of him and settled down for a tense, uncomfortable flight.

Shortly before we landed, the flight attendants came round with the necessary landing cards. I took out my passport and pen and began to fill mine out. The large man next to me seemed to be having a problem with his and after a few minutes he indicated by hand movements that he would like help. I asked him to give me the card – still taking care not to look him in the eye or inadvertently touch his hand – and started to write down his details. His accent was hard for me to decipher but he spelt out his name and I managed to catch his date of birth.

Next, I asked him where he was born. I enunciated my words very carefully, hoping he would understand my English, but I simply could not make out what he said in reply, though I asked him to repeat it three times. Finally, he pulled out his passport – and to my surprise it was a British one, identical to mine! As I opened it to find his place of birth, I heard him speak again, in a broad Scots accent: 'I wis born in Glasgae.' I almost fell off my seat laughing! He told me that he ran a corner shop in that city. He turned out to be a kind and gentle man who was more than willing to guide me through the complex immigration system at Delhi Airport.

What a lesson for me not to judge people on appearances! I thought I was sitting next to a radical cleric, or even a 'jihadi', and I was actually sitting next to a grocer from Glasgow. I hope I learnt that lesson well.

14

This Is My Holy Book

Word about our teams seemed to get around international mission circles and it wasn't long before we were asked to help out in another emergency – only this time it was the result not of natural disaster but of war. In July 2006, two Israeli soldiers had been captured by Hezbollah in a cross-border raid. Israel responded by bombing and shelling southern Lebanon, and Hezbollah fought back with rockets. Tens of thousands of people had fled north to Beirut, seeking safety and peace.

The grounds of Beirut Bible College became a refuge for displaced families and the staff soon realized that they would need medical help. Their initial request to RB was simply for doctors and I was confident that we could send a team. The next request was more problematic: Could we send people who were not North Americans, or at least didn't look North American? There was a lot of anti-US feeling in Lebanon at the time because of that country's support for Israel. It meant we would have to seek volunteers from among our Ecuadorian staff. The final request was: Could the people we sent all be women? The people displaced from southern Lebanon were mainly women and children and it wouldn't be appropriate for male doctors to treat female Muslims.

I thought this might be a tall order, but I started asking my friends at Hospital Vozandes, mainly women who specialized in general practice, whether they would be willing to go to a war zone. I was careful to point out that we would actually be far away from the fighting. Despite my doubts, a team was assembled within a couple of days. Three GPs, a general medical doctor and a gastroenterologist – all Ecuadorians – would go with me. (Thanks to the dark hair and dark skin I so resented as a child, I blended in very well!) Four of them were fairly fluent in English, so we would be able to work with Arabic-to-English translation. I was excited to be making this trip with some of my closest friends. I was looking forward to an adventure – I didn't realize just how nerve-wracking it would turn out to be!

Driving through the streets of Beirut a few days later, we were all struck by the beauty of the city. Its wide, palm-lined avenues, pastel-coloured buildings and plentiful coffee shops reminded me of southern Spain or Italy. We especially appreciated the Lebanese food that was served for breakfast in the hotel where we stayed the first night – bread and olives and hummus (which is not widely available in Ecuador) eaten alfresco. It was hard to believe that we were in a country at war.

Our Lebanese hosts were kind and gracious. Before long, they asked us the question they had obviously been desperate to put to us: Would we be willing to go to the south to help people in the area that had been bombed? A ceasefire was now holding, a UN peacekeeping force had been deployed and they felt that we would be welcomed by the communities close to the border, who would be able to see from our appearance that we were from a neutral country. They were confident that we would be safe there – and the medical needs there were great.

Once again, my valiant Ecuadorian colleagues accepted the challenge and agreed to go wherever they were needed; and so it was we found ourselves driving down the coast road towards the border with Israel. The journey was beautiful. We admired the ports of Sidon and Tyre, which the apostle Paul refers to in the book of Acts. Our hosts had promised us that we would be able to stop and see the sights on the way back, and also visit the famous forests whose cedar trees had long ago been used in the building of Solomon's temple. We were excited to be seeing places mentioned in the Bible and to be going where heroes of our faith once walked.

Our initial destination turned out to be a small Druze village in the very south of Lebanon. The Druze are an ethno-religious group whose faith is, loosely, a mixture of Islam with a generous dose of Gnosticism. They don't proselytize because it's impossible to 'convert' to their faith – you're born a Druze and you die one.

We would be staying in a large rented house where we enjoyed the hospitality of a wonderful woman from the USA called Kaye. She spoke Arabic and normally worked in another Middle Eastern country which I can't identify, but had come to help in Lebanon by hosting the teams of aid workers that were coming through. A young couple from the USA who were working locally were going to be co-ordinating our work schedule.

The first evening, Kaye gave us an introduction to the country, the people and the area where we would be serving. She also invited us each to tell of our faith journey and we had a precious time of sharing and prayer as we reflected on the ways God had brought us all to that place at that time. Our team bonded all the more tightly, and in the days that followed our friendships were strengthened by our shared experiences.

Each day, we held clinics in different places. Evidence of the Israeli air-raids was everywhere. They had bombed with precision, taking out houses they believed to belong to Hezbollah activists and leaving others right next to them unscathed. In some areas, barely one building was left standing. We were shocked by the scale of the destruction – though Hezbollah had already begun rebuilding and it was obvious that help was available for those who had lost properties.

We were shocked, too, by the way the raids had affected the children in the villages. When they heard an aeroplane passing high overhead, they rushed out to pull us into hiding with them, making signs to us that planes mean bombs. They were terrified as they looked up at the sky and it was sobering to see their distress.

Most of the people we treated were coming in for routine things. Many had lost their homes and so had also lost their prescription medicines, for diabetes, high blood pressure, heart disease or whatever, and they couldn't get more because there were no shops open. Coupled with the extreme stress and trauma they were experiencing, they were desperately in need of our care and the medicines we'd brought with us. We saw people suffering from angina and chest pain, anxiety, insomnia, breathlessness and symptoms of panic attacks. Sometimes, however, the best thing we could give them was our time. We sat and listened to their stories, gave them our attention, empathized and sometimes cried with them, too.

One Sunday, we were invited to go to church. Although Lebanon is a predominantly Muslim country, it has a large Christian population which is often overlooked by the outside world. (In fact, Lebanon has eighteen recognized religious groups. The seats in its parliament are divided equally between Christians and Muslims, with specific allocations to the Maronite, Melkite and Armenian Catholics, the Eastern and Armenian Orthodox, the Protestants, the Sunnis, the Shias, the Alawites and the Druze. There is an unwritten rule that the country's president must be a Maronite, the prime minister a Sunni and the speaker of the parliament a Shia. The hope is that with power apportioned in this way all the different communities will coexist peacefully.)

After the service, the local believers set out a banquet for us all to share, a feast of roasted lamb, green salads, tabbouleh, bread and olives and a host of other delicacies. Perhaps the most popular part of the meal was the dessert. Lebanon is famous for its deliciously sticky sweet pastries covered with honey and dusted with toasted almonds. The best-known is baklava but we discovered that there are many variations!

As we took our leave later that day, one of the women said to me anxiously: 'Please tell people about us! Please don't forget us! Tell them there are Christians in Lebanon! All Christians pray for Israel, but we, too, have been "grafted onto the olive tree". Please ask people to pray for us as well!' Her words struck deep within my heart: 'We, too, have been "grafted onto the olive tree"' – she was referring to Paul's metaphor in Romans 11:17 that non-Jews become part of the body of Christ by being grafted onto the 'olive tree' of God's chosen people. We must not forget to pray for Christians in places like Lebanon.

The Lebanese people were wonderfully welcoming to our Ecuadorian team. There is no history of conflict between the two countries – in fact, many leading Ecuadorian politicians have had Lebanese roots, including two presidents, Jamil Mahuad and Abdala Bucaram. There seems to be an affinity between the two peoples and I believe that this made the Lebanese we met feel relaxed and confident talking with us. They saw me, I perceived, as 100-per-cent Ecuadorian.

We attended to everyone who came to us for treatment, including members of Hezbollah. (In fact, we were all given badges with the Hezbollah symbol on them as a mark of appreciation for all we had done for the local people, though I've never had the courage to wear mine in public!) So open to us did these people seem to be, we felt free to leave some Christian literature in Arabic in the places where they waited to see the doctors.

One day, I went out to the waiting area to call the next patient and saw a beautiful young woman in a traditional black robe and a sky-blue head covering intently reading one of the booklets we'd put out. It was her turn to see the doctor, I knew, but I waited until she had finished it before calling her.

The doctor in question was Ximena. The woman spoke good English but Ximena doesn't, so I was translating for her. I don't recall what the woman's complaint was, but I do remember that we had a good conversation with her. She seemed very open and we spent a lot of time just talking with her, sharing our experiences of life and getting glimpses into each other's backgrounds. I felt a strange sense of a bond between us and before she left I asked her if I could give her something that was precious to me. 'I hope you can accept this,' I said, handing her a Bible in English and Arabic. 'This is my holy book. I hope you'll read it.'

She took the Bible from my hands and held it to her heart and then kissed it. Then, she gave it to her mother (who had been sitting in a corner of the room, unable to understand anything we were saying) and she did the same. As they left, I knew that this young woman held in her hands a book that contained the words of eternal life. I have never otherwise, before or since, had an opportunity to give the Scriptures to a Muslim believing that they would actually read them, but that day I prayed – and believed – that (as Isaiah 55:11 puts it) God's word would not return to him empty but would achieve the purpose for which he sent it.

Another day, we went to a town called Deir Mimas, right on the border with Israel, whose soldiers we could see patrolling on the other side of the barbed-wire fence. Deir Mimas had been heavily bombed and some parts of it had been almost totally destroyed. Buildings lay in ruins, the walls still standing were very unstable and much of the town was deserted. The building we had planned to use for our clinic had been damaged, we were told, but an alternative venue had been found.

To my surprise, we were taken to the mosque, where a side area had been set up for us. We took off our shoes, covered our heads and got to work, though it felt strange to be doing so as the call to prayer echoed around us and men gathered nearby to kneel and pray. I never cease to be amazed at the way God opens doors for his people so that, through the Holy Spirit, we can incarnate his presence in some of the unlikeliest places on the planet!

Our time in Lebanon was by now drawing to a close. We had finished most of the work assigned to us and had only a couple of villages left to visit. Among the highlights of our trip, we agreed, had been attending to some of the Syrian Bedouins who come to Lebanon each year for the olive harvest. They had made us very welcome in their comfortable tents and treated us to wonderful food and tea. It was a truly special experience! We had also enjoyed several meals in the UN peacekeepers' camp. The soldiers in our area were predominantly Spanish and they had been thrilled to have a group of lovely Ecuadorian women to chat to in their own language.

One afternoon, towards the end of our stay, we decided to walk down from the house into the nearby village to buy some souvenirs. Ecuadorians are generous present-givers and they would never return home from a trip without gifts for the whole family. The women adore gold jewellery and someone had told us that Lebanese gold is especially fine and pure, so my colleagues decided that earrings, chains and bracelets would make perfect presents for their loved ones.

The owner of the jewellery shop must have thought it was his lucky day as five foreign women pored over his wares. (I am neither a great giver of presents nor a great appreciator of gold – I prefer silver – so I didn't join in the pawing!) Finally, everyone was satisfied with their purchases and we set off home. It was beginning to get dark as we left the shop and hurried down the street.

As we walked along, we became aware that something was up. People were shouting and running in the street and small crowds had gathered outside those shops that had a television in the window and were craning their necks to get a better view of the screen. We tried to work out what was going on, to no avail – but whatever it was, it was clearly not good.

Suddenly, a van drew up alongside us. Kaye was sitting beside the driver and she yelled at us to get in quickly. As we were driven at speed, alarmed by her obvious anxiety, back up the hill to the house, she explained that a prominent Christian politician had been gunned down in Beirut. Pierre Gemayel had been a popular figure and already protesters were massing in the streets of the capital. The situation throughout the country could turn very nasty, she feared.

Her instructions were to send us to Beirut immediately before roadblocks made travelling impossible. A driver would be arriving shortly to take us. We were to go to a particular hotel in the Christian sector of the city and not venture outside its walls.

We threw our clothes into our suitcases and tearfully hugged her goodbye. Within thirty minutes, we were on our way, confused and upset by this abrupt ending to what had been such a wonderful trip. We were fearful of what awaited us and anxious about how we would get out of the country and back to Ecuador. I was especially concerned. As the leader of the team, I had a responsibility to care for my colleagues and ensure that they got back to their homes and families unharmed and on time, and I now found this a heavy burden. I prayed all the way to Beirut, begging God to keep us safe both on the road and in the days ahead.

We entered the city by a roundabout route. The hotel that had been chosen for us sat on a high hill overlooking the city, surrounded by extensive gardens. The staff were extremely kind and courteous, but their faces betrayed their fear of what the future might hold in store for their city and their families.

That night, we all slept fitfully. There was a sense of unease in the air that was almost palpable. I checked in with my principal contact with RB, a good friend of mine called Yvonne Kennedy. She is based in Spain, which is only an hour behind Lebanon, and she had been asked to make contact with me every day and inform the mission of any problems or concerns. She prayed with me over the phone and we agreed to stay in touch throughout the day. The hotel staff reminded us not to go outside the grounds of the hotel. They were expecting massive demonstrations during Gemayel's funeral, which could easily turn violent.

We spent the day talking, resting and walking around the gardens. We tried to keep an eye on the television to monitor the situation in the city centre. Our contacts in Beirut said they would tell us what we needed to do and when. By the evening, we began to relax a little. The funeral had passed and everything appeared to be calm. We were due to fly home the next day. I was flying via Rome with one of my colleagues, Susie Alvear, and the other four were going via Paris and Amsterdam, to Bogota and then on to Quito. As we had an early start, we all decided to turn in.

By nine o'clock, most of the team were asleep. I was preparing to go to bed when my phone rang. It was Yvonne. 'Sheila,' she said, 'Muslim militants have taken the main road to the airport and now it's blocked. You won't be able to leave.' This was bad news. I decided to talk to the hotel management to see what they knew – fortunately, they spoke some English. They tried to reassure me. They said they would keep me informed but they didn't believe we would suffer serious inconvenience as the security forces were working to take back the road and reopen the way to the airport.

Shortly after, they called me down to reception again. We needed to be gone by 3 a.m. to give us the best chance of getting through to the airport, they said. The road was open again, but they feared that the militants would retake it before long.

I consulted Ximena, who was my 'second in command'. Should we wake the others and tell them what was happening? We decided to let them sleep – there was nothing to be gained from sharing our anxieties with them. We had a long journey ahead of us and they needed some rest. Ximena and I stayed awake and prayed.

At 2 a.m. I woke the rest of the team. 'There's a problem,' I told them. 'We have to leave now.' Nobody panicked, nobody protested, nobody demanded more information. Each one quietly and calmly got up, packed her things and was ready to walk out the door at three.

As we left reception, the hotel manager himself came to help us into the van that had been sent for us. We piled in, making sure that our heads were completely covered. He explained that our driver would be taking a longer route to the airport but that it would be safer. He also said that if the van was stopped, none of us should speak – we should leave it to the driver to deal with things. Before we pulled away, I saw the driver praying. The manager looked anxious as he waved us off. I didn't know what kind of danger we might be in, but all my instincts were telling me that this was not a good situation.

The tension in the vehicle was thick. Nobody spoke. Our normal chatter and banter were silenced – we were all deep in our own thoughts and prayers. My heart seemed to be jumping out of my chest and I tried to calm my breathing as we sped through the dark and unfamiliar streets of Beirut. We were all asking God for safe passage to the airport and beyond. I knew that Yvonne, too, was spending the night in prayer.

After what seemed like an age and a thousand miles, we saw the airport lights in the distance. Within minutes, we were being waved through the first checkpoint. Finally we pulled up outside the terminal. For some reason, I didn't feel we would be safe until we were inside it, so I urged everyone to move quickly. We said a hurried goodbye to the driver and, breathing a huge sigh of relief, took refuge inside the building. There we all hugged each other, laughing with relief to think that within a few hours we would be leaving behind the conflict and chaos of the Middle East and heading back to beautiful Quito, with its green mountains, snow-capped volcanoes – and peaceful people. The stories we would have to tell them when we got home!

An hour later, Susie and I were in the air, dozing as Alitalia carried us to Italy. The adrenalin rush had gone and exhaustion had set in. Landing at Rome on schedule, I switched on my cellphone and was perturbed to see a number of voicemail messages from Yvonne and Ximena awaiting me. At once I started thinking that something terrible must have happened in Beirut. Had the airport been attacked after we'd taken off? I was seized by panic.

When I eventually got through to Ximena, she told me they were back at the hotel. Everyone was fine, she assured me, but the airline had not let them board. Ecuadorians are allowed only one stop in Europe without a visa and their return journey would have had them touching down in Paris and Amsterdam. I told Ximena I was going to buy a ticket straight back to Beirut, but she soon made it clear how pointless that would be. Sometimes I have this 'saviour complex': an overdeveloped sense of responsibility – or pride, really – that makes me think I'm the only one who can fix things. I'm grateful for honest, straight-talking friends who can put me in my place – and Ximena is one of them!

Beirut seemed to have calmed down, she told me. In fact, they were going to venture out to see the city. Our partners had been in touch and Air France was arranging tickets for them to fly to Paris the following day and then direct to Bogota. God was taking care of them nicely and he didn't need my help.

She was right. God was indeed taking care of them, far better than I could have done. The next day, they flew to Bogota – on the top deck of a Jumbo, business class!

On reflection, I can see that that whole trip was an exercise in trusting God, in every department of life. The six of us have reflected together many times since on our experiences in Lebanon. Our patients got good treatment. We cared for the sick, the poor and the homeless. We encouraged the down-hearted, we wept with those who had suffered loss and comforted them in their mourning. But maybe the biggest impact had been on each of us. Our shared experience had forged a bond between us all. Our faith in God had been strengthened and our trust in him had grown. And our lives had been truly blessed and enriched by the people of Lebanon.

15

Speaking Life

Not all of our ministry opportunities in challenging places are due to war or natural disaster. RB staff have been privileged to help in many places where there was simply a need for well-trained doctors or nurses. One of these is the Republic of the Congo (Congo-Brazzaville).

A young doctor from New York called Joe Harvey had a vision to set up the first Christian hospital in Congo-Brazzaville and in 1999 he and his young family moved to Impfondo, a town in the remote north-east of that country. It stands on the bank of the River Ubangi, which at that point forms the border with the vast, war-torn Democratic Republic of the Congo (DRC), formerly known as Zaire. The Aka pygmies and the Lingala-speaking Bantu people hunt and grow crops in the dense forest there, which is also said to be the home of a large, dinosaur-like creature known locally as *Mokele-mbembe* or 'one who stops the flow of rivers'.

My first visit to Impfondo was in April 2005. RB had received a request to install a radio station in the hospital once it was up and running and Lee Sonius, our regional director for sub-Saharan Africa, made the long journey to take a look with me. (RB had sent me to look at various ministries on that continent and assess where we could offer help and support.

Apart from Congo-Brazzaville, I also visited Ivory Coast, Malawi, Kenya and South Africa.) Miriam Gebb, another missionary nurse, came with us for the sake of propriety, as mission policy dictated, as Lee is a married man.

There is no road to Impfondo and it's accessible only by plane, flying twice a week, or by riverboat from the capital, Brazzaville, which takes roughly ten days. We chose the former. We boarded an ancient prop plane and it rattled and shook its way up-country, apparently following the river. We were relieved when we landed safely two hours later.

We spent a delightful few days with Joe and his family and staff. Everyone was working hard to convert a former communist youth-training camp into an operational hospital. Old buildings were being renovated, the encroaching rainforest was being cleared and pathways laid and gardens planted. Carving a place of healing out of such dense vegetation was clearly a daunting task, but Joe believed fervently that God had commissioned him to take it on and that sense of calling gave him strength and courage to complete it.

Furthermore, he believed that God was meeting all his needs, beginning with the donation of the property by the government and the provision by Samaritan's Purse of a shipping container full of medical equipment and supplies. He could see God's hand in every detail – and so, in spite of a multitude of setbacks, he held on firmly to what he believed were God's promises to him.

Our visit lasted only a few days but we promised to return when Pioneer Christian Hospital was open and a broadcasting licence for the radio station had been granted. Over the next two years, Joe kept in contact and we followed his progress closely. We heard wonderful stories of patients with seemingly hopeless conditions being restored to health and strength and of a growing body of Congolese believers who were following Jesus.

Most of the time, Joe was the only doctor on the staff. On his shoulders alone rested the responsibility for the patients and the administration and maintenance of the hospital, as well as relations with government officials and compliance with the often complex rules and laws that governed a place such as Impfondo. Eventually, the pace of life, the volume of patients and the stress of practising medicine in such a setting began to take their toll and he desperately needed to take a lengthy break in order to rest and recuperate. However, there was no one to relieve him, and so he wrote and asked me to look for medical staff to help out.

Whenever I went to a conference or met doctors or nurses or administrators who were thinking about serving in mission, I would mention the need in Impfondo. I looked especially for French-speaking staff (as French is Congo-Brazzaville's official language) – but always without success. Finally, I wrote to him: 'Joe, I can send Spanish-speakers from our hospital in Quito to cover for you, but I can't find anyone else.' He responded quickly, telling me that he would find interpreters.

So it was that in 2006 RB sent a succession of Ecuadorian, US and German staff to run Pioneer Christian Hospital while Joe, its solitary doctor and administrator, took a much-needed year off. One of the Ecuadorian doctors we sent, Paulyna Orellana, had dreamt of serving in Africa her whole life. She had worked in the Oriente and had also served the Afro-Ecuadorian peoples who live on the river systems in the north-west of the country. She was trained in both general practice and surgery and knew how to do both in very basic conditions.

She stayed in Impfondo for six months, acting as medical director as well as being the only doctor on the staff. She picked up enough Lingala and French for basic conversation and relied on her interpreter for more complicated consultations. One of the amazing things we discovered was that in the seventies and eighties, when the country was under communist rule, many Congolese had been sent to study in Cuba and had learnt Spanish there. So, finding translators turned out to be quite easy. It was certainly not hard to see God's hand in *that* detail!

Towards the end of her stint in Congo-Brazzaville, it became apparent that the burden of her responsibilities and the strain of being far away from her close-knit Ecuadorian family had taken their toll on Paulyna. Like Joe, she was now tired and stressed. I decided I would go to Impfondo to help her finish up and then accompany her home. I thought I could support her on the journey, particularly through the airports in Brazzaville and Paris, which are each in their own way eccentric and confusing. I had no idea what an ordeal my own journey would be!

The flight from Paris Charles de Gaulle was uneventful enough. The Air France plane was new and spotlessly clean, the cabin staff were attentive and the food was rather delicious. Disembarking at Brazzaville was a shock, however. The heat, the noise and the smell almost caused sensory overload and I began to perspire freely as the humid air enveloped me. The crude concrete terminal buildings seemed dirty and uninviting. People in a variety of uniforms were swarming around, shouting and waving papers. Everyone was yelling, in fact. It was pandemonium.

I looked for the baggage carousel but there wasn't one. After twenty minutes or so, a truck drew up and the bags were hauled out and piled in the middle of the floor. Then the frenzy began as people struggled to retrieve their luggage. Actually, most of the passengers entrusted this task to one of the men standing around for this purpose. These would dive into the fray and emerge from time to time with a suitcase or holdall that vaguely answered the description they'd been given. There was much shoving, tugging and arguing about which bag belonged to whom. I realized that I had little chance of getting my case without help.

I knew that someone had been sent to meet me, so I looked around anxiously for a white face or a sign with my name on it. Eventually, I spotted a Congolese man holding up just such a sign. By this time, sweat was running down my back, my hair was plastered to my head and I knew my face was red with the heat. I desperately wanted to get out of that oven and into some fresh air. I introduced myself to him – his name turned out to be David – and he explained that once he had got my bag he would drive me to the guest-house in the city where I was to stay the night.

Nine hours or so later, after a fitful sleep but a good breakfast, we set off again for the airport. My hosts at the guest-house had given me four numbered, sealed envelopes which they said I would need to hand over to various people at various times during the check-in process. My ticket had been purchased and that was in the first envelope. I was taking some supplies up to the hospital, and the money for the excess baggage was in the second one. David took me through the immigration process – perhaps because it's so remote and the border with the DRC is so porous, Impfondo is treated almost like another country – and that was another envelope. Finally, he said he could go no further but I was to give the final envelope to the policewoman at the door of what passed for a departure lounge and wait in there for my flight to be called.

I thanked him for all his help and bade him farewell and he promised to be there to collect me and Paulyna on the return journey. I pushed the door to the 'departure lounge' and went in. It was a large room with rows of plastic chairs and a clear view of the aircraft lined up on the tarmac outside. There was a door to the toilets on the left – but actually the whole room smelt like a toilet! Again, it was unbearably hot, without the slightest movement of air.

I took a seat and waited. The time for my flight came and went. Periodically, an unintelligible announcement would come over the Tannoy and people would get up and move towards the exit onto the tarmac to board their plane. I concentrated hard on these announcements but could never make out what was being said. I was afraid I would miss my call, so each time the Tannoy squawked I would look around hopefully, waving my boarding pass and asking, 'Impfondo? Impfondo?' A tall Muslim man in a spotless white robe was sitting in the row behind me and kindly he took it on himself to answer my desperate question each time. '*Non*', he would say and wag his finger.

Over the course of the morning, many planes took off to who knows where. Most of them were ancient Russian Antonovs with their distinctive drooping wings, which looked as if they hadn't seen any maintenance in a long while. To pass the time, I checked out all the aircraft on the tarmac and graded them on how decrepit they appeared to be. I decided I wanted to fly in the one that had a lion painted on the tail – it certainly looked the nicest.

Eventually, another garbled announcement was made and I thought I heard the word 'Impfondo'. I turned to my friend in white. 'Impfondo?' '*Oui*', he said and we both got up and walked out onto the tarmac and up the stairs into the plane. Of course, it wasn't the one with the lion on the tail.

Many African airlines provide 'free seating', which means that passengers are free to choose where they sit. This arrangement causes a stampede from the terminal to the plane, with a great deal of jostling and shoving to get the best places. The interior of this particular aircraft was decorated with tiger stripes and the seat covers likewise were orange and black, which looked almost psychedelic. The air-conditioning was not working and I was already bathed in sweat as I found myself a window seat.

I could see suitcases and packages being loaded onto the plane. The cargo hold was evidently full and sacks of coconuts, oranges, pineapples and mangoes, heads of bananas, boxes and bags were all being stowed inside the cabin. I fumbled for my seat belt and to my dismay discovered that it had no buckle. By this time, a large woman had taken the aisle seat next to me and the plane was almost full, so I had no alternative but to tie the belt in a knot to secure it across my lap.

Never a very confident flier, I found this disconcerting. I began to worry even more as the propellers started to turn and still no safety briefing had been given. As I have said before, my brother is a pilot and so I know the importance of seat belts and safety procedures! I was beginning to feel *very* anxious.

I decided to do my own briefing and looked for the nearest emergency exit. The red exit sign was barely visible behind all the piled-up baggage. I guess that was one of the reasons why there was no briefing. I prayed and committed the journey to God, asking that underneath would be his everlasting arms (as Deuteronomy 33:27 puts it) and quoting Psalm 121 to myself for comfort:

> I lift up my eyes to the mountains –
> where does my help come from?
> My help comes from the LORD,
> the Maker of heaven and earth.

I reminded myself that God is my help, my shield, my protector and comforter, even in the scariest times. Then, I settled down for the two-hour flight.

The plane was clearly overloaded as it struggled to clear the trees at the end of the runway, and it continued at a very low altitude for the first half-hour. After a while, I got out a book to read, to try and take my mind off things. Within minutes, I noticed a faint smell of petrol. I sniffed. I sniffed again. Unmistakably petrol – but where could it be coming from? I began a dialogue in my head. There could *not* be a smell of petrol on a plane. I must be imagining it. I tried to ignore it, but the smell only got stronger. Finally, I decided I must have an acute case of phantosmia, an 'olfactory hallucination'. I certainly hoped so!

By now, the atmosphere in the cabin had changed. Passengers who had been asleep were wide awake and talking to each other loudly and pointing. The large woman next to me started to elbow me in the ribs and point and shout: '*L'essence, l'essence!*' My heart began to race in panic as I pulled out my French phrasebook and looked up the word *essence*. There it was: 'petrol'. I leant over the woman to see what she was pointing at. To my horror, a trickle of liquid was running down the aisle.

'Oh no,' I thought, 'I'm going to die – in a plane crash in deepest Africa, all alone and far from everyone I love! Lord Jesus, please help us!' I called out in my heart. 'Protect us! Save us!'

By now, all the passengers were panicking and yelling. A flight attendant appeared as if from nowhere – actually, he'd been playing cards at the back of the plane – and began to search through all the luggage piled up in front of the emergency exit. Finally, he found what he was looking for: a large chainsaw with a leaking tank. He removed it to the back of the plane, wiped up the petrol on the floor and then served everyone a drink.

To my amazement, within ten minutes the other passengers had gone back to sleep. Calm was restored. I tried to make sense of the fact that twelve hours earlier I had been on a plane where nail clippers and bottles of water were prohibited, while here, in Congo-Brazzaville, leaking chainsaws were allowed on board!

I was glad when we landed and I was reunited with Paulyna. She had fitted well into Impfondo life and was obviously much appreciated by the hospital's staff and patients alike. I was impressed by her progress in French and Lingala. It was also evident, however, that she was exhausted and ready to leave. Within three days, Drs Eckehart and Klaudia Wolff would be coming from Ecuador to relieve her. Eckehart is a general surgeon who also does orthopaedics, while his wife is a paediatrician who would be helping with anaesthesia. Both of them worked in our hospital in Shell.

Paulyna was now winding up, and there were various events to mark her leaving; but she still had to manage the general running of the hospital right up to the moment when the Wolffs arrived at the door. The day before our departure, we were gathered with most of the staff having morning devotions and the daily report when suddenly one of the Congolese nurses ran into the room, greatly agitated. A rapid conversation in Lingala ensued. I could tell that Paulyna caught some of it by the look of concern that came over her face. She jumped up from the table and called to me in Spanish: 'We have to go, we have an emergency. Hurry up! You're scrubbing up to assist me.'

I was caught completely off guard – sometimes I have to remind myself that this is what I was trained for. As I ran after her, I told myself: 'You can do this, you're a nurse!' We hurried through the hospital grounds to the operating theatre and Paulyna explained that a woman from way out in the forest had come in bleeding. She was heavily pregnant and the nurse suspected she had placenta praevia. This is where the placenta is growing in the wrong place and blocks the birth canal. If labour begins, the placenta can rupture and then not only the baby but the mother, too, is likely to die.

It sounded to us as if that was exactly what was happening. As we changed our clothes and scrubbed up, we learnt that the mother had seven other small children. Her husband was outside, pleading with us to save his wife. Paulyna assured the theatre staff she would do everything she could for her – they told her the baby was already dead.

Surgery started and proceeded quickly. Within minutes, a blue scrap of humanity had been delivered. Then the complications started. The woman began to haemorrhage. Paulyna tied off blood vessels, cauterized and swabbed in an attempt to stem the bleeding and find out where it was coming from. We worked together well. I was able to anticipate what instrument she would need next and have it ready to slap into her hand so that she barely had to look up from what she was doing. The nurse anaesthetist, a local man called Siko, kept us posted on the woman's vital signs. Her blood pressure was dropping as she had lost a huge amount of blood – it was all over the table, the floor and us. How could she possibly survive?

We worked faster. I prayed: 'God, help us! God, stop this bleeding, *please*!' After ten tense minutes, it eased and the woman's blood pressure started to increase as the intravenous fluids flowed into her veins. We slowed up and Paulyna was able to take more time to examine where the blood was coming from and what else she needed to tie off. I found myself with a free hand, so I started to flick the baby, a little girl, to see if there was any response. I touched her, began to massage her. She did look dead – she was navy blue. Her lungs had not expanded to take in oxygen. There was no first breath, no cry.

As we continued to work on the mother, I occasionally reached over to slap the baby gently. Once when I glanced across I noticed she was no longer navy blue but purple. 'The baby's alive!' I yelled. Before our eyes, to our astonishment, she turned from purple to pink. A nurse rushed over to her, dried her, cleaned out her nose and mouth and continued to massage her. Within minutes, we heard the sweetest sound: a baby crying! I wept. I laughed, I was so happy. She was alive!

When mum and baby were tucked up together an hour later and we were cleaning up the theatre, I remarked that I never thought the mother would survive, let alone the baby. Siko looked at me and said: 'I did. In this hospital, we speak life, not death. We see God give life in miraculous ways like this every day.' I felt humbled and chastened as I realized that, with all my dependence on Western civilization and technology, I had overlooked the God of miracles, who really is the only one who gives life.

The next day, we visited mum and baby before we left. Paulyna Sheila was doing very well – and Mum was making a good recovery, too!

At the airport, the immigration officers took my passport and refused to return it, even though the plane was waiting for us, until we had given them some money. After that, the flight back to Brazzaville was a lot less stressful than the flight out – in spite of the cargo of live crocodiles that was being taken to the capital for meat. The creatures had their jaws taped shut and we were assured they could not escape from behind the netting that held them in the back of the cabin. I tried not to think about the possibility of the plane landing in Brazzaville with some enormously fat crocodiles and no passengers.

16

The 'Ecuador Team'

I had begun to think of myself as an experienced disaster-relief worker – but that was before a massive earthquake hit Haiti in 2010. Everything I thought I knew and was prepared for became as nothing when I was faced with the immensity of that disaster.

My office in the loft of my home in Tumbaco is one of my favourite places. My desk is positioned so that I look out at Pichincha, the 4,784-metre volcano that towers above Quito. I often find myself gazing at its majesty when I should be working. It was at that desk that I was sitting that evening in January when a short e-mail arrived in my inbox alerting me to what had happened. A quake reaching 7.0 on the Richter scale had been quickly followed by two powerful aftershocks of magnitude 5.9 and 5.5. The epicentre was roughly 15 to 25 kilometres from Haiti's capital, Port-au-Prince.

I switched on the television and tuned to BBC World News, where there was continuous coverage of the unfolding story. The confusion and uncertainty surrounding the situation were evident. At 8 p.m., Port-au-Prince lay in total darkness. Nobody really knew the extent of the damage. Initial reports said that most of the city, which was home to 2.2 million of the country's 9 million inhabitants, had been destroyed. Hundreds of thousands of the world's poorest people had been living there in makeshift dwellings in unplanned shanty towns. Nobody could even guess at the number who were dead or injured.

Haiti is roughly two-and-a-half hours by air from Ecuador. It occupies the western end of the small island of Hispaniola. The larger, and prosperous, Dominican Republic lies to the east, a haven for holidaymakers seeking the white beaches and crystalline waters of the Caribbean Sea. Haiti is one of the poorest countries on the planet. According to the World Bank in 2012, almost three in five of its inhabitants live on less than $2 a day. According to the UNDP in 2013, one in four live in 'extreme poverty' on less than $1.25 a day. There is, reportedly, only one doctor for every four thousand people.

At that point, however, I knew little about Haiti or its chronic problems. I knew only that a catastrophe had happened, almost literally on our doorstep, and we needed to be ready to respond. I called my friend Jordan Lycan, who covered Latin America for Samaritan's Purse. She was already working on a plan. I told her I could assemble a medical team and she said she would call me back. Next I rang Wayne Pederson, the president of Reach Beyond, to get his formal approval, which he duly gave. I then made several calls to our medical staff to see who might be willing and able to drop everything to fly to Port-au-Prince.

By the time I went to bed that night, I had a team that I could lead to Haiti. Only one place still needed to be filled – I had to find another orthopaedic surgeon. I didn't know how we would get there or where we would work, but we would be ready to go the very next day.

As soon as I arrived at my office in Hospital Vozandes early the next morning, I rang the medical director to ask whether we had an orthopaedic surgeon he could release for the trip.

Since we were likely to be flying into and out of the USA, they would need a US visa in their passport. The medical director said he would check with the head of orthopaedics, a doctor called Leonardo Febres – and almost immediately Dr Febres rang me. He could go himself and yes, he had a visa.

Samaritan's Purse called and confirmed that our team was needed. They told us to fly to Miami, rent a van and drive to West Palm Beach, where a private jet would take us to Port-au-Prince. We were needed at the Baptist Mission Hospital on the outskirts of the city. Accommodation was available for us. We learnt that every hospital bed was full and that patients were lying in the corridors and even in the grounds of the hospital waiting for help. The situation was critical. Electricity had failed throughout the city, water was in short supply and supplies of diesel fuel for generators were running out. Thousands of people were dead, thousands more were severely injured and hundreds were still trapped.

Our team gathered to pray. Eckehart Wolff, I knew, would be a key player. He is a surgeon from Germany who is able to improvise with whatever material is available. He is also a decision-maker – as the old adage has it of surgeons, 'often wrong but never in doubt'! He was accompanied by Dr Paul Barton, the anaesthetist from our hospital in Shell. It was to be a challenging experience for him – it would stretch him as well as exhaust him in every sense. Steve Nelson and Marcos Nelson – not related – were our GPs who would help to care for the post-op and general patients. Dr Febres would be working with Dr Wolff, while I would be the only nurse on the team! Finally, I'd invited Martin Harrison, a fellow Brit, to be our general dogsbody. Apart from the menial work of running and fetching, he would also take photos and talk to the media, make daily reports to our various offices in Ecuador, the USA and the UK – and deal with any problems we had in getting water. Martin is actually a water engineer – in Ecuador, he had been working on our clean water projects – and his skills in that department proved to be crucial in the days that followed.

We left Quito early the next day, at once both excited and apprehensive. The news reports were giving a very grim picture of the situation in Port-au-Prince. The death toll was far greater than originally thought and services were overwhelmed. Not least, the airport could not cope with the number of planes arriving with search-and-rescue teams, supplies – and journalists!

We landed in Miami, quickly cleared customs and immigration and boarded our rented van for West Palm Beach. We stopped en route for lunch, including Ramen noodles. It's become quite a joke with our teams that my answer to the question of sustenance is always Ramen noodles. They may have very little nutritional value but they are light to carry, can be tasty and do stave off the pangs of hunger. The WHO stipulates that disaster-relief teams must be self-sufficient in terms of water, food and shelter and must not be a burden in any way to the country they have come to serve. In the end, however, the forty packets of noodles we bought in Miami were used by the hospital, because Samaritan's Purse brought in cooks and proper food to feed the teams that were working with them.

At West Palm Beach airport, we were joined by a pleasant group of logistics specialists and a camera crew who were all with Samaritan's Purse. Their task would be to document what was happening on the ground and work out a plan for that organization's short- and mid-term response. Sitting together in the lounge of the private jet terminal, we watched on television the scenes of devastation in Haiti. I was particularly shocked by an interview of a young girl from the USA, who told of being literally pulled from under the wreckage of a house. Her leg was crushed and later had to be amputated.

The reality of what we would soon be facing began to hit home. Dr Wolff reviewed over and over again the quantity of Steinman pins he had packed to deal with complicated fractures. Dr Barton worried about the availability of anaesthesia equipment. The two Dr Nelsons discussed what kind of medical supplies would be needed and what we had brought. I worried about all of the above and also the safety of the team, since aftershocks or even fresh quakes were always a danger. We spent a lot of time praying about all these things.

Time dragged as we waited. The plane was fuelled up and ready to go, but the airport at Port-au-Prince and the surrounding airspace were closed for safety reasons. The volume of air traffic had overwhelmed the system and permission to land was not being granted. We were anxious to get there and felt frustrated because we knew we could contribute to the relief effort. As the afternoon wore on, the television continued to show harrowing pictures from Haiti but it became clear we wouldn't get there that day.

Word came early the next morning that we could leave – immediately! We grabbed our gear and headed to the airport, where the plane was ready for take-off. We piled into the executive jet that had generously been lent for the relief effort, admiring its plush white leather seats, its polished mahogany surfaces and its opulent bathroom with scented soaps and soft towels. Before we took off, we paused to pray for the people of Haiti. We prayed for those injured, those trapped, those bereaved, and those afraid. We prayed for ourselves, for strength, wisdom and safety and that we would have many opportunities to show God's love to the people we met. Then we tried to relax and prepare our hearts and minds as we watched our progress across the Caribbean on the video screens.

Two hours later, we were approaching Hispaniola, crowding around the windows to see what things looked like from the air. Even though we were still some distance from Port-au-Prince, we could see the devastation. The city appeared to have been flattened. As we descended, we could make out groups of people waving frantically at us as they stood close to what must once have been their homes. It was clear that in the outskirts of the city and the countryside around it supplies of water, food and shelter were urgently needed.

Our landing slot at the airport allowed twelve minutes for the plane to be unloaded and take off again. We knew that this would require 'all hands on deck' and almost as soon as the tyres touched the runway we were ready to go. Someone flung open the doors and dropped the steps and quickly we formed a human chain to unload the supplies and the rest of our cargo. Everyone worked hard and within nine minutes the plane was emptied, turned around and ready for take-off.

As it disappeared into the clear blue sky, we were left at the side of the runway with a huge pile of bags, boxes, cases and cartons. There appeared to be no customs, no immigration, and no baggage handlers. We commandeered an ancient flatbed trolley we found rusting nearby and piled it high before pushing and pulling it towards the terminal. It took our combined effort to make it move. The heat was stifling and by the time we reached our destination we were all dripping with sweat. We were very glad to see someone waiting there to take us to the hospital.

The thirty-minute drive there allowed us to get a glimpse of the state of the city. Even though we skirted around the centre, where the greatest destruction was, we were shocked to see piles upon piles of rubble, which rescue workers and locals were picking apart, searching for signs of life. Cars lay crushed under buildings which had simply pancaked on top of them. The smell of death and decay already filled the air. Trucks full of bodies were making their way out of the city to what would become mass graves. Everywhere there were people, walking aimlessly or standing in huddled groups or, more purposefully, digging in the wreckage. It was clear they had no homes to go to, although by now 'tent cities' had sprung up, with makeshift shelters made of plastic sheeting and cardboard as well as proper tents.

The Baptist Mission Hospital is in a nice area of Port-au-Prince, set a little above the city within its own grounds. It was founded by the Southern Baptists and had a largely Haitian staff. There was accommodation for these on site, as well as a small Bible school and a church. In normal circumstances, the campus must have been a pleasant place to live and work. Not now. My first impression was that everywhere was simply *full*. There were injured people everywhere. Every bed was filled, and some had two or even three people in them. The floors were covered with injured people. They were lying in the gardens, camped out with their families. The offices were full of injured people, on the desks, the tables – even in the cupboards. It was overwhelming. Where on earth would we start?

As we picked our way through the mêlée, desperate people rushed up to us, waving X-rays, seeking help for their loved ones, pleading for our attention, shouting for us to see *their* mother first, to attend to *their* baby, *their* child, *their* brother – surrounding us, crowding us so we could barely move. It was total pandemonium.

We managed to find some of the exhausted staff, who had been working heroically without a break for three days, many of them not even aware whether their families and friends were still alive or their homes still standing. The pain they had suffered from all they had seen and felt was etched deeply into their faces. They told us of the battles they had fought and the carnage they had witnessed.

As is customary in such societies, the medical director tried to make a speech to welcome us; but he broke down after a few words, exhausted and overwhelmed. His Haitian staff began to weep as they told us they had been praying for so long for us to come and were so grateful we had finally made it. After they'd given us a very quick tour of the hospital, we sent them to whatever remained of their homes and families, assuring them that we would figure out what to do and where to start.

That was easier said than done. We headed to the operating theatres to find out what was available. There were two of these, of which one was only partially equipped and the other was almost empty – it seems the missionaries had been focusing on the Bible school and under normal circumstances the hospital had been doing only five or six operations a week. The good news was that there was equipment for giving general anaesthetics and some full oxygen cylinders. There were also vast quantities of sterile drapes ready, some intravenous fluid, a limited range of surgical instruments, a decent operating table and adequate lighting. We decided to move all the best equipment into one of the rooms to make a halfway decent operating theatre where we could concentrate our efforts efficiently.

Dr Barton stayed to organize things while the rest of us went to 'do rounds' and see whether we could draw up a list of priority cases so that we could begin surgery as soon as possible. We had already detected the ominous smell of gangrene as we walked through the hospital. Crushed and broken limbs lacking blood supply were already necrosing and would need swift amputation if we were to save the patient's life.

We tried to work quickly but the sheer number of patients, the complexity of their conditions and the need to work through interpreters ate up the afternoon and we decided to make a start on our list of people most urgently requiring surgery and finish the rounds later. However, the two GPs would continue seeing patients and they would try to pick out those they felt were most urgent.

So, we started. We prayed with each patient before they were put under anaesthetic and asked God for his help and his hand of healing on them. Once again, we depended on him for wisdom and strength.

I was the circulating nurse, which meant that I had to hand to each of the surgeons whatever they required next, properly sterilized. Ideally, I was supposed to anticipate their needs before they had even voiced them. I summoned up every last scrap of theatre knowledge I had gained during my training and everything else besides I had learnt on the occasions I had scrubbed up for surgery in Ecuador. Nonetheless, I was ill-prepared for the severity and complexity of the injuries we were dealing with. I had never seen a limb being amputated before, for example, and I was flummoxed by requests for things like 'bone wax' (which turned out to be a product of beeswax that is used to seal bones after amputation to prevent them bleeding).

Sadly, amputation was one of the procedures we had to perform most often. It is always a last resort, and especially in a place like Haiti, where prosthetics are hard to obtain, but many of our patients had limbs so badly crushed that it was impossible to wire them back together. There were other complications, too – toxins build up when the blood supply to an arm or leg is cut off and, once it is restored and they are released into the circulation, they can cause shock and damage the kidneys. Other fractures were open and exposed, filthy and already infected. At one point, I remarked that we weren't seeing any head or chest injuries and Eckehart replied: 'Those are the ones who didn't make it.'

We worked long and hard into the night, but the list of urgent cases only continued to grow. Eventually, Dr Barton called me to one side. He was exhausted, emotionally and physically. 'We have to stop,' he said. 'I can't do this safely any more, I need to rest.' Eckehart thrives on hard work and is simply tireless, he loves to operate and can go on for hours without a break – but his team couldn't match his energy and stamina. So, it fell to me to call it a day. We decided to sleep for a few hours and then start early again the next day.

The rest of the time we spent in Haiti now seems like a blur in my memory. Hundreds of patients passed through our operating theatre. The children were the hardest to cope with. Many of them were now homeless and others had become orphans. It's hard to amputate a child's arm, knowing that many years of disability lie ahead – but it would have been harder not to do it, knowing they might not survive.

A few people and events stick in my mind. Every morning we were greeted by the smiling, wrinkled face of Madame Cafa. She stood about four-and-a-half feet tall in her theatre scrubs but she proved to be a spiritual giant as she joined us in our morning prayers, pouring her heart out to God in Creole on behalf of her people. We didn't understand her words but we certainly understood her passion and knew what was in her heart. She worked all day without resting to provide sterile drapes, towels and instruments for the surgery. She was there when we arrived each morning and she was still there when we left each night, exhausted. She hugged us, loved us and tried to encourage us when things were just too hard to take.

After three or four days, she asked us whether we had a blanket she could take. By that time, supplies were coming in and we had been giving out blankets to the patients. Of course we had one for Madame! The interpreter questioned her a little more about her needs and we learnt that this beautiful, selfless, Spirit-filled woman in her eighties had been sleeping in a car since the earthquake. She had lost her home and everything in it, and yet she was more concerned for others than for herself.

Someone else I cannot forget was a woman in her late thirties who had actually been in the hospital before the earthquake awaiting surgery for a gastrointestinal haemorrhage but had somehow got overlooked in the sudden rush. She needed a transfusion first, because her haemoglobin levels were so low, but we had no blood and no blood replacement products. Eckehart knew that without surgery she would surely die, so he lay down and donated a pint of his own blood. He then got up and operated on her. Marcos Nelson attended to her post-op care and stayed with her continuously for a couple of days. Sadly, she didn't make it. Her death affected us all deeply.

There came a point when we finally felt we were getting on top of the operating list. We started to talk of spending more time on post-op rounds and maybe even getting to some of the more infected cases. Maybe we could even ease up a little? No way. Some US soldiers came to the hospital and said they had some patients who needed surgery. Eckehart told them bluntly not to send anyone unless they also sent supplies. Within hours, the first truckload arrived and once again we were swamped with work!

At every moment in every situation we were aware of God's sovereignty. He is the giver of life and also, ultimately, the One who takes it back. People we thought would live died and people we thought could not be saved miraculously survived. We worked equally hard on both.

Outside the operating theatre, people were being saved in a different sense. A team of pastors from Samaritan's Purse visited the patients as they lay in their beds, counselling, comforting and praying with people who had suffered so much. They told us that many came to faith in Jesus Christ, renouncing their previous faith in voodoo.

Other reminders of God's presence came in practical ways. The city's electricity supply had been knocked out by the earthquake and at the hospital we were relying on generators. Already we had siphoned the diesel from every vehicle we could find and now we were down to our last few gallons. We were told we would probably run out completely by mid-morning. We pared down our operating list for the day – no way did we want to be halfway through an operation and find ourselves with no light and no monitors. Imagine our surprise and delight when, at about 11.30 a.m., a tanker drove up to the hospital and filled up all the diesel tanks! We had no idea who sent it or where the fuel came from, or who else even knew about our plight, but we knew that God did and that he is Jehovah Jireh, which means 'The Lord will provide' – and he certainly did!

Likewise, the hospital was running out of water. Normally, only a quarter of its beds at most were full and then the city's water supply was adequate; but in the days following the quake it was running at 50 or 100 per cent *over* capacity and the theatre was in use 18 hours a day – besides which, the grounds of the hospital had almost become a refugee camp. The general lack of water in Port-au-Prince posed a serious threat to public health, and indeed cholera broke out ten months later and many died.

Samaritan's Purse had shipped in a couple of huge water filters, but its technicians were having difficulties working out how to install them and where to source the water. However, Martin figured out how to draw the water from a muddy duck pond in the hospital grounds through a filter to provide an abundant supply pure enough to drink. It was amazing how long that duck pond lasted us!

A few days later, more help started to arrive. A medical team from the USA came to help at the hospital, accompanied by a senator who was also a surgeon. It was such a relief to be able to share our responsibilities and also to take a little time for rest! However, the first day they joined us in theatre I was horrified to see one of them washing a filthy wound with some of our precious sterile water! I glanced across at Eckehart, who just shook his head and gave me a look that told me to bite my tongue. The senator did his best but unfortunately his speciality was cardiothoracic surgery, which was absolutely no use to us. He had to call on our help with one particularly complicated fracture and he and his colleagues were horrified when Eckehart produced his Steinman pins and the ordinary household drill he was using (swathed in sterile cloths and with properly sterilized bits) and proceeded to wire the bones back together!

After that, the US team stood back for a few operations and just observed. They saw how we used clean, not sterile, water to wash filthy infected wounds before applying the sterile iodine solution commonly used for skin prep. They saw that a drill is a drill and as long as the parts touching the patient and entering the bone are sterile it doesn't matter what kind of drill it is. They saw how our team worked together, how Eckehart helped to clean and mop the theatre after each operation, how we prayed with our patients and their families, how frugal we were with our instruments and our supplies. They saw how we loved each other, encouraged each other and helped each other. They saw how sensitive we were to each other's needs – for quiet, a kind word, a drink, some food, a rest. At the end of that first day, they told us all they had seen – and they prayed with us and thanked God for 'the Ecuador team'.

I make no apology for being proud of that team. They worked selflessly and fearlessly even as the ground beneath us continued to shake and the hospital walls swayed with the aftershocks. They wept for their patients, prayed for them, comforted them and rejoiced when the outcomes were good. They gave of their skills, their time and their very selves – even their blood!

When the time came for us to leave Haiti, we knew we could never be the same again. We had seen so much suffering we would never forget, and we had seen so much courage. We had seen God act in so many miraculous and unexpected ways, healing bodies, healing minds and changing hearts. I believe that he is building his church in Haiti, calling out a people for himself from the darkness of voodoo. He is preparing his bride and he will come back to receive her one day, spotless and without blemish. In the meantime, he graciously still has work for us to do!

Landing in West Palm Beach and seeing the clean, white beaches, the turquoise sea, and the palm trees swaying in the breeze, and feeling safe, it hit me hard. All we had seen and done and felt, the horror, the terror, the suffering, the loss – I could barely hold back my tears. I wanted to weep and wail, to shout, to curl up on the floor. But it wasn't yet time for that. Many of the others who shared our flight were home, as the US Red Cross welcomed us all with cookies and hugs and water and fruit. We still had one more plane to catch.

Late that night, as we walked out of customs and immigration into the arrivals hall at Mariscal Sucre International Airport in Quito, I heard a huge cheer go up. Colleagues from Reach Beyond were waiting with flowers and fruit, banners and cameras. Hugs and tears. We were home and safe at last.

17

Through It All

When I was at Bible college in the late 1970s, there was a song that was popular with the students. It seemed that everyone was singing it – maybe it had something to do with the fact that you needed to know only three basic guitar chords to play it. It talks about life's difficulties, journeys taken and experiences shared, both high on a mountain top and deep in the valleys. The words of the chorus are:

Through it all,
Through it all,
I've learned to trust in Jesus,
I've learned to trust in God.
Through it all,
Through it all,
I've learned to depend upon His Word.[3]

I think that neatly sums up my experience of life up to this point, except that I don't think I *always* trust in Jesus – sometimes I am afraid. Nor do I always depend on his word – though when I do, my heart is stilled and comforted. Nonetheless, my trust and dependence are growing the longer I walk with him.

As I have reflected on the stories I've told in this book, I really wanted to finish with some profound theological insight, a nugget of wisdom or a word of exhortation that would thrill you and challenge you and inspire you to go out and change the world. But all I can find to say is: God is faithful. He can be trusted, not always to do what we want, but to do what is best.

He has a plan for each of our lives and it's probably a far better one than we can imagine. He still takes damaged people and starts to rebuild them, and then uses them to tell other damaged people about him. He is faithful and he meant it when he said he would never leave us. He truly does provide for our needs. He will always be with us. He loves us and will never give up on us.

God is so gracious that he invites us to work alongside him. He commissions us to do something important for him – to tell the world about him. He doesn't use only the rich and the famous, the wise and the clever to do this. He takes ordinary people leading ordinary lives – indeed, weak and vulnerable people – and he empowers them to do extraordinary things. That is his plan for us: for me, for you.

He gives us one life to live and he challenges us to live it 100 per cent for him and his kingdom.

And God always, always, *always* knows what I'm doing here – wherever that may be.

Author's Note

The cover photo was taken in West Africa. Crowds of people were gathered under the trees waiting to see the doctors at the rural clinic. Children were playing all around.

African children are usually the happiest children in the world. Despite having very few material possessions they laugh, they sing, they play with whatever is available (even fashioning toys from plastic bottles), they dance – and they smile.

This little girl caught my eye. She was so solemn. She would not smile – not even when Dr Steve tried to tease a smile – he is usually 100-per-cent successful. She did not smile, even for him.

When Dr Susie examined little Grace, as she is called, she diagnosed protein-calorie malnutrition. Described as "the sickness the baby gets when the new baby comes" or "the disease of the deposed child"[4]

Grace was being raised by a neighbour, as her mother had gone to the city to work. Basically, Grace was undernourished, swollen – and sad.

Reach Beyond's local partners were able to contact Grace's mother who came to the village a couple of days later. She was unaware that Grace was not receiving the right kind of food. Grace went to live with her grandmother. With a good diet, she made a complete recovery.

We learned that Grace, or Amazing Grace as we call her, is now in school and doing well – and yes, she smiles. A lot.

Notes

1   Samuel T. Francis, 1875. 'Oh the Deep, Deep Love of Jesus.'
2   Elisabeth Elliot, *Through Gates of Splendour* (Milton Keynes: Authentic, 2005).
3   'Through It All', Andrae E. Crouch. © Copyright 1971, Renewed 1999. Manna Music, Inc./ASCAP (admin. By ClearBox Rights). All rights reserved. Used by permission.
4   Jennifer Stanton, 'Listening to the Ga: Cicely Williams' Discovery of Kwashiorkor on the Gold Coast'. Clio Medica: Studies in the History of Medicine and Health. 61: 149–171.

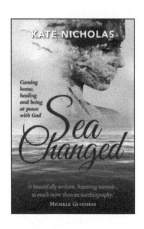

Sea Changed

*Coming home, healing and
being at peace with God*

Kate Nicholas

'I wanted to know how God could love my father yet
allow him to suffer such despair, but no one could give
me a satisfactory answer. God seemed very distant and
lacking in empathy . . . so, in anger, I turned my back and
walked away . . . I knew only one thing, that I had to keep
on travelling until I found the right direction.'

Kate Nicholas's vibrant autobiography allows us to
follow her on her travels in search of faith and truth –
from Aberystwyth to London, through Asia to Australia,
from the US to Africa – and watch her discover a loving,
healing God.

978-1-78078-162-4

Authentic

We trust you enjoyed reading this book
from Authentic. If you want to be informed
of any new titles from this author and other
releases you can sign up to the Authentic
newsletter by contacting us:

By post:
Authentic Media Limited
PO Box 6326
Bletchley
Milton Keynes
MK1 9GG

E-mail:
info@authenticmedia.co.uk

Follow us: